SECRECY

=

SUFFERING

The Hardships of Hiding

SECRECY

=

SUFFERING

The Hardships of Hiding

By Dennis Meredith

SMOKEBLOOD PUBLISHING
Casper, WY

SMOKEBLOOD

This book is memoir. It reflects the author's present recollections of experiences over time. Some names and characteristics have been changed, some events have been compressed, and some dialogue has been recreated.

I would like to thank the real-life members of the family portrayed in this book for taking me into their home and accepting me as one of their own. I recognize that their memories of the events described in this book are different than my own. They are each fine, decent, and hard-working people. The book was not intended to hurt the family. Both my publisher and I regret any unintentional harm resulting from the publishing and marketing of *Secrecy = Suffering: The Hardships of Hiding*.

ISBN-13: 978-0-9600491-2-7

Library of Congress Control Number:
2019940544

Published by S M O K E B L O O D Publishing
Casper, WY | smokeblood.com
@_smokeblood

Cover design and layout by Colt McMurry
Cover design © Smokeblood, 2018
Edited by Marissa Waraksa @mariesa_faer

Printed in the United States of America

I dedicate this book to all those people who have ever lived with secrets.

To those of you who've ever hidden something from your family, your friends, your coworkers, the world… hiding, because you were scared that your secret revealed would cause you to be treated with disdain, disappointment, or even fear. Leaving you unaccepted, alienated, scorned, mocked or even physically damaged.

This book is for you. I see you. I hear you. I *understand* you.

I can, and will tell you, first hand, of how painful and difficult it is to hide who you really are from the world. Something about living in secrecy deeply damages the human spirit, wounding and winding the soul in ways unnatural, and ultimately shattering.

I will tell you this: Do all you can to live authentically. Do the work to process and own your pain, your fear, your trauma; because I promise you *it is so worth it*. An unparalleled self-empowerment greets the courageous - those who fight to live their lives through absolute authenticity.

To live with such transparency is, in and of itself, profoundly healing and fully liberating. I have found my freedom, and I know *you can find yours*.

To *you.*

CONTENTS

"If you want to carry a positive action,
you have to first develop a positive vision."

-Dalai Lama

FEAR AND LOVE

Living your truth can feel like fear. Like pain. Or merely like a deep, dark tunnel you know you don't want to go down, even if you don't know why.

Alienation from the self means alienation from the world. If you find yourself unable, or feel it unsafe, to open your heart fully to living in your authentic truth, you aren't really living. You deserve to engage fully with the world around you, without fear. Each and every one of us is worthy and deserving of living our own truth.

Simply as we are, we are a perfect expression of human goodness. Of nature. We are each but a branch on the great, expansive tree of life.

Each of us, unique; each of us worthy in our faceted, individual expression. The world and its illusions merely cloud our view to our own inner landscape, causing us to cling like cotton candy to unsustainable ways of living.

Codependency, cowardice, malice, resentment, victimization, and other forced imbalances line the surfaces of the walls we build up around ourselves in an attempt to keep the world out. But we can't keep the world out. We must find the courage to thrive amidst it.

I know, though, of the gripping effects of fear, and of how it steals your courage. In the heat of the dark night, I have been engrossed in its shadow, unable to see through to my own inner light - even when it was already lovingly present, revealing the pathway for me.

Heck, I'm a pastor, to a modest African American congregation in the south, and there were times in my journey where I found it near impossible to see the light clear enough, even in the telling of my own sermons.

I hope for my story - of fighting through the darkness out into the light of truth - to help you take steps towards liberating your own. Towards freeing your voice, and letting your heart shine brightly on this beautiful planet.

I, as example, was not always open about my life.

I didn't feel safe speaking my truth, or in living in line with my heart's true desires. I felt only fear.

Once I stepped through that veil of fear, and chose to live, I realized that all that fear was only a mirage of my own making, and that I had, in fact, always been free to make the choice to step into my full self. To *love* my whole self.

The journey since has been one of ecstasy. For, no matter the challenges that have surfaced since, I knew deep down of how I was strong enough to navigate through. I knew I was capable, that it was worth fighting in order to live, and thus that there was no outcome or event clever enough to steal my light away from me. It was my choice.

Regardless of the truth in your heart, you miss out when you live in disdain of your own inner truth. There is such a sense of empowerment to be found in the arrival of one's true self. There is power in standing strong as yourself amidst a world of variant light and shadow. You are the only judge and jury to your self-perception; to your freedom, no matter what the physical world seemingly tries to cage you within.

You are not a victim to this world. I am not a victim, and even when I have seen myself as a victim, I was not a victim. Society's norms change continuously - what is banned one day, is allowed the next - and there is no one to owe explanations to for your choices, other than your **self**. What seems to cage you, you can free yourself from. In fact, no one can release you from your chains *except* for you.

Each person faces an individual plight. Aloneness is nothing to fear, for it is truth. However, so is it truth that we are all connected, and the things that make us unique - that seemingly separate society - do not actually create boundaries and walls by themselves. Only we can do that. Only we do.

I found myself fighting through torrential downpours, hurricanes, tornadoes, and never in the still of the eye. No; rather, whipped around by the confusion of fear. The frustration it enlivens.

You are strong. This I promise you. And you're probably a hell of a lot stronger than you think. You can find your way through the gripping emotions and physical pains of not living your truth.

This journey from hiding your voice from the world (and yourself), to emancipating your truth and fully embodying who you were meant to be all along, can be a varying experience for each one of us. Perhaps we find ourselves wrapped up in our minds, thinking the worst of ourselves, and holding our perceived *lack* responsible for what *isn't* the way we wish it were. Maybe we feel trapped, and think someone can help us, when truthfully, they cannot. They can only guide.

Find the courage to see things as they really are. Your pain is valid. And very, very real. However it has affected or contorted your life, it is worthy of compassion.

Your suffering, on the other hand, is shaped by you. To love yourself now, in this moment, is to love your past, and all the wounds that have scarred your spirit. To love your wounds is to use them as gifts in healing your self, and in healing the world.

Don't stifle your pain. **Share it.** Witness it. Learn of how it has helped you, taught you, guided you. Allow the truth to justify your pain. Learn from my struggle. Truly, this is why I share *my story* with *you* today.

Homophobia exists absolutely everywhere, even in the gay community. I've experienced it my whole life.

I think of the stories… the ones that have haunted my consciousness ever since I first came across them. The stories of others' experiences; the ones what ended in tragedy.

When I was young, another young man from my neighborhood was beaten to death by a group of four guys around the same age.

When the young men who had committed the crime stood before the judge, only three of them openly expressed their remorse for what they had done. One of four, however, did not seem to feel the least bit remorseful for his crime.

When the judge asked him why he did not seem remorseful, he informed the judge of how his pastor had said in a sermon, "God hates gays." He felt like he was helping God, by eliminating the homosexual individual.

There was another young man growing up; another distressing story. This young man's body was found in the trash. It was not a story that made the news headlines. No. But it was a story that made its way into the many living rooms of our community.

Adults and young people throughout our neighborhood were discussing the death of the young man, James, who was commonly known as the 'sissy boy' of our community. There were others who were gay as well, but not openly, nor as flamboyantly as James. When James's body was discovered, it was as if a message was sent to the whole community: "If you don't want to die a horrible death and embarrass your family while you're at it, you'd better not be openly gay around here."

I know I was influenced greatly by these instances. Although no one in my direct circles, growing up, ever gave me the feeling that I should fear my true nature - my natural feelings - the memories of these events haunt me, to this day.

While living in the midtown area of Atlanta as an adult, I once met a transgender male who was engaged in prostitution. We fell into an open conversation about why she was on the street, prostituting. Upon hearing her story, it took everything in me to hold back the tears:

She had been put out by her father at thirteen years old. She moved in with her grandmother, who then passed away when she was fifteen. She lied about her age to get a job at a grocery store, to pay the bills to keep her grandmother's house. The income was not enough to sustain the upkeep of the home, however; so she tried to go to school and work at the same time. A friend of hers then introduced her to a lifestyle of receiving fast money through the selling of her body. She embraced her options.

While listening to her story, heartbreaking as it was, I attempted to offer her the opportunity to come to my church, as it is a safe space for trans and gay people. My offer to come to the church was not received very well; unfortunately, because of the fact that her father - whom had put her out of his house at thirteen - was a minister. She was living as a street-worker to survive. This street-worker is one of thousands of young people strewn across this nation whom have been rejected by their families, and do whatever they can to make a living.

There is no shame in making the most of the hand you are dealt. Nor should there ever be! But I know of how it can feel so defeating, when there are parts of the world - dark corners of each community - where homophobia is more of a rigid restraint, than a hindrance. Where numerous lives are left abandoned, because of the individual truths they choose to lead.

Of course, then there are the countless men across the African nations who are harmed, jailed and killed for being gay, every single day. My heart aches for the hundreds of gay people around the world whose lives are put in danger for living their truth.

No matter the struggle, it's difficult to stand up for oneself. Whether it's kids on the playground calling you names and throwing things, or an elderly lady on the bus exhibiting her disdain for your adult relationship without remorse, it can prove difficult to handle the situation with love, from the heart, rather than stoop to the level of the bully.

Especially as blind anger fills your eyes with blackness, and you start throwing punches into the darkness of loneliness and deprivation, your soul can scream without you even knowing why.

Heck, and the older you are, there's no extra ease to be found. At least, not unless you carve it out for yourself, by choosing to send compassion to those who persecute you. Not unless you can see their pain clearly, and understand how no one who lives in love would ever harm you, much less judge or criticize your actions. And that, the only way out is through: No matter the discomfort a situation presents, knowing that to choose to stand up for your truth by directing loving *compassion* towards those who try to shame you, is the only way to help the world heal.

I've experienced racial and homophobic slurs my whole damn life, from childhood to the present day. Though as a child, I really didn't understand what *homophobia*, nor what homophobic comments, really meant, I could still feel the rage, fear and frustration in the voices of those who delivered the messages.

I cannot recall anyone I lived with, in my family, who actually used any homophobic language while I was growing up. As a matter of fact, I hadn't even heard the word 'homophobic' until I was grown; probably not until my early forties. However, even as a child, you just *know* the words when they're used to indicate people who are gay or same-sexed. You can feel the shift in tone, suddenly understanding the message that their behavior was somehow unacceptable, if they were called 'sissies', 'nancies', 'daisies', or any other variation of 'flower'.

By the seventies, Flip Wilson 'came out', and would constantly flip his hand back and forth to indicate whenever someone was gay or 'funny'. I can remember hearing my parents and the other older people say to one another, "Well, you know, so-and-so is *funny*", which meant that they were gay; they were same-sex attraction. But there wasn't a whole lot of it around; only amidst 'polite conversation' here and there.

I grew up with three brothers, my mother and father. And, you know, my brothers and I would tease each other saying things like, 'you're a sissy!" whenever someone wouldn't do something, but it wasn't out of viciousness. It was never. I didn't grow up where homophobic language was vicious or meant to really demean people. I wasn't directly exposed to any language that indicated that to be same sex was demonic. I just wasn't around it.

But still, there was enough context in the social interactions of my childhood days to let me know that being gay was not something you went around talking about openly. It was something best kept private. Where, in today's society, this homophobic language is more common; where kids are so often openly bullied and called gay and there's even suicide - and I'm sure there probably still was back in the fifties and sixties - but when I was young, it just wasn't something that was so out in the open, where people were publicly attacked, as they are today.

Back then, you knew someone was gay, or that someone was referring to another person as gay because of the subtle inferences around what they said, but it was never overtly attacked by - at least, not by my - church, family, or community. I don't know if it was just because of the community I had grown up in, or whether it just wasn't a part of the open kind of consistent dialog of my community, but it wasn't there.

All in all, I can't say how, exactly, I came to terms with knowing that it was wrong to be gay. How I had come to assimilate what people were saying. I guess, for me, I felt the same way about sex with women. That it, too, was wrong - that is, unless you were married. I had gathered the message growing up that sex, in general, was not something you do, regardless of who you do it with. I never particularly thought one was worse than the other.

The message was, *Okay, I'm not supposed to be doing this. I am not supposed to have sex with women or with men because I am too young and unmarried.* It was all based upon the biblical idea that if you weren't married, to have sex of any kind was fornication. There was no delineation, nor mention, of same-sex attraction that stood out to me as a child, or even in my adolescent years growing up.

I didn't really grow up in a judgmental family, to be honest. I mean, we had our problems - many though they were. But I'm often around people nowadays who talk about how they'd grown up in these critically judgmental families, where their parents were super religious, and imposed these biblical standards. What they had interpreted the Bible to say, they imposed on their children. I didn't grow up like that. Even though I went to church. It was not a part of my community or family, and so I didn't experience that kind of persecution. What I see now, in today's society, was no part of my upbringing.

What was a large part of my upbringing was my low self-esteem. I struggled most of my life against it. I've struggled to see myself as worthy of love, often feeling that I *knew* there was something wrong with me, and even with the light of God's love, ever-present as it was in my life, found myself in constant struggle with whether I was truly deserving of that love, or whether I, alone, for my faults, was not.

If you struggle with low self-worth, the decisions you make in life will all filter through that sense of self-worth. Your perception of yourself shifts the reality you perceive. The more you question your worth, and fear either being too much or not enough, the more your experiences in the world will dig into that same perspective. Negativity, self-pity, and self-eradicating inner dialogue will only breed more of themselves.

Good, bad or indifferent, your self-esteem will have a great deal to do with the choices you make. Choices led by low self-esteem are not healthy - not to mind, body, or soul.

What many in religious communities call 'sinful acts', and demonize people for, are usually simply a projection of their own sense of low self-esteem. For an example, if you are a promiscuous person, it may extend from low self-worth. From an imbalance in the inner landscape, that need only be given attention and love to heal. To label the promiscuity as sinful, or pass judgment on the individual based solely on this aspect, only compounds the person's sense of low self-worth, and stands only to drive the behavior in deeper, repressed and shamed.

The truth is, however, that you choose your own experience. You choose your adventure! You can choose to take that shame, that pain, or that negative internal dialogue, embrace it with gratitude for being a part of your journey, and then throw it in a sixty foot hole in the ground. You can give your pain back to nature. She'll recycle it. Or compost it. Or, at least, do *something* better with it than you can.

Find that inner love - strengthen it like the strong, beautiful muscle that it is - and use it like a shield to protect you against any arising enemies.

I've learned a lot from my pain. I've learned a lot from paying attention. Embrace your pain; don't run from it. Embrace how what hurts you actually defines your own, personal truth. And then, be courageous in how you use that truth out in the world.

By perpetuating love from within your own heart, you need not seek it from the world without. You need not place your empowerment in the hands of others, and can learn how to love yourself into the life of your dreams - the life you are meant to live!

Most importantly, embrace yourself. Embrace your flaws as important facets that make you who you are, and love them into oblivion. I promise you they're there for a reason - at the very least, they're there to make life more interesting! Nowadays, if I begin to judge myself, I chuckle at my mind's nature. I know better than to let negative thoughts permeate my reality any longer.

I am no longer crippled by fear. I let it wash over me, and carry onward, following the inner voices of strength and resilience that have carried me through so much. I no longer cripple with anxiety, doubt or worry about my choices. I know I am perfect just as I am, because if I can survive through all that I have so far, then there's no way I am *not* a direct expression of God's love; of his grace. And no matter what you believe, or believe in, it doesn't matter, so long as you find the faith and *hope* to persevere through the challenges that come your way, and to *always* speak *your* truth.

No matter where you are on your path, know that you are always on the right one, no matter how ragged its paving, so long as it's moving you closer to living a life that brings you joy. A life full of hope; a life where you feel no guilt, no shame, no self-criticism, and are never choosing to stay in feelings of fear.

I promise you that the courage already exists within you to handle anything in your life, and to always choose to push past fear as it arises, softening into choosing whatever option most aligns with compassion. Compassion will out, and I find it always takes you closer to having everything your heart so deeply desires. Closer to living life authentically, fully embodied, honest and free.

Read onward, dear friends, to hear of my story, humble though it is. I have "failed" more times than I can count, yet through the patient act of loving myself - regardless of how stupid I can get, or how my choices led me down dark and narrow alleyways - I always made it out alive. And I was always grateful, in the end, for these deviations that only led me closer to walking in the light of my true nature.

ONE

THE EPIPHANY

My whole life came to a screeching halt when the doctor said to me, in September of 2009, at fifty-six years old, *You are in the fourth stage of cancer.*

There is no fifth stage.

There I sat, in that uncomfortable, bleach-white office as my doctor filled me in on the details of the various tumors that were persistently growing and spreading all over my body, even as we spoke - in my back, my abdomen, my neck, and under my arm. He also explained to me how the only way we would be able to get rid of the cancer - Hodgkin's Lymphoma, by the way - was to do a systemic cell transplant. Thing was, there was absolutely *no guarantee* that stem cell would completely eradicate the cancer.

Now, I had already been diagnosed, back in January of 2006, with Hodgkin's Lymphoma, but thought I was scot-free from the chemo I had gone through at that time. I guess I was wrong.

In this stem cell transplant, what the doctor told me they would do was remove some of the stem cells from my bone marrow or blood, freeze them, and then give me some extremely high doses of radiation and/or chemotherapy to kill the remaining cancerous cells. After which, they would then thaw and reinsert my own [hopefully cancer-free collection of] stem cells back inside of me, replacing the ones that were destroyed.

The issues with this process include the high chance of going through the entire thing, only to have your own still cancerous cells put right back into your body, leaving you basically back where you started. Another includes the possibility of regrowth, as your immune system is generally the same one as before the transplantation, or a worse version of itself, and one that cannot necessarily sustain a healthy environment to support healthy cellular growth. All in all, with this information, I didn't feel very hopeful of my chances.

As I drove off from the doctor's office, all I could think was, *This is it for me. I am going to die.*

My mind raced, full to the brim with images of all the faces; of all the people I'd gone to the hospital and prayed for over the years, who'd been fighting against some form of cancer that wanted to attack their body. So many of whom I stayed beside as they took their final breath....

These memories tripped me up the worst. *I didn't want to die.* Their bodies had looked so withered… eyes bulging, lips parched, breathing deeply like they were going through a long tunnel. I remember feeling the weight of their breath, as it slowed with sadness. Soon, that tunnel would surely bring them to the end of their lives.

I began to think to myself, *What have **I** left behind? What is the world going to remember me by? Have I really made an impact on the world?* Somehow just being a preacher, pastor, father and husband didn't seem sufficient. I had wanted - had *hoped* to make more of an impact, and feel the purpose of my life drench my heart with wholeness…. But I didn't. As I drove home from the doctor's, all I recognized before me was what I hadn't yet done. What I hadn't yet become. The potential I had hoped to fulfill, that now sat hopeless on the sidelines of the cancer I was sure would rule my life until my final breath. I felt so scared, and alone, and… *insufficient.*

I mean, I knew and acknowledged how devotedly grateful I was for what I *did have*… what I *had already become.* A father to three wonderful sons whom I loved and adored with every fiber. A pastor to three reverent churches: Mt Zion Baptist Church in Birmingham, Alabama, Mt Calvary Baptist Church in Oakland, California, and now the great Tabernacle Baptist church of Atlanta, Georgia.

But what had I done in my life so far that was different than any other father out there? Different than any other Baptist preacher?

You parent your children. You're there for them absolutely whenever they need you, no matter what. You sacrifice selfish desires, and do what you can to lend them all the wisdom you've collected over your own years. You love them with your *absolute* whole heart.

Then you lead your congregation. You go to your pulpit every Sunday, bringing with you a soul-stirring message. The members shake your hand after church, gracing you with their gratitude for the moving sermon you just delivered. You feel strong, surrendered, and purposeful in your efforts. And yet, none of this seemed to say to me, *You are ready to die, because you have completed your life, and fulfilled your destiny.*

I had hoped to fulfil a greater purpose with my days. I had always felt like I was moving towards fulfilling something... something so deep; something I couldn't quite describe or know in advance how to prepare for... I only knew I had always been waiting and moving towards it. Call it destiny? Call it purpose? Call it a devout calling from God; a purpose greater than I alone could benefit from.... No matter, this cancer seemed like the ultimate roadblock that would stop me from answering these questions in my heart; from uncovering the deep longing calling me from within.

That night after the doctor's visit, I couldn't sleep. I prayed through the night. At one point, I had remembered this particular passage from the bible: Just as a king of Jerusalem was about to die, he turned his face to the wall and prayed, and thus, God granted him fifteen more years to live. I thought, perhaps, even though mine was a literal interpretation, that so devotional of a surrender to what God had in store for me was exactly what I needed to do. At least, with where I was, and what I was feeling, it didn't seem it could hurt to give it a try. So I did.

As I prayed my way through the remaining night, I fell into a deep, deep sleep, and had an epiphany. My deep, internal longing finally spoke up, and said to me, *If you want to live, you have to commit to being an advocate for the marginalized, the alienated, the underserved, the underprivileged, the demonized and the dehumanized lesbian, gay, bisexual, transgender, and questioning population of the world - the LGBTQ community.*

Here I was, finally ready to fulfil my purpose. I had finally become quiet enough to listen to, and receptive enough to hear, my destiny's call. To coordinate the pieces of my life into a configurable puzzle, using my personal lessons learned to positively uplift the collective. Finally ready to do absolutely whatever it took to fulfil my true, devotional purpose. I had finally, completely surrendered. Had finally *Let Go, and Let God* lead me like a shepherd does his sheep.

There are inner *yesses* and *no's* within us all. Sometimes these are more difficult to decipher, confusing themselves amidst the emotional turmoil that springs forth from the varying elements of our everyday lives. But sometimes, our inner acceptance and resistance shout at us with the clarity of their message, and this was inarguably one of those times. For me, the strongest I had ever experienced.

My path, somehow through the confusion and fear of my cancerous revelation, had become clearer than ever, and ready to reveal itself. My purpose felt now like the firmest foundation I'd ever held beneath my feet. I felt strong in the revelation I had experienced.... I knew God was now integrated fully onto my path, which I know was because I had decided to finally and *absolutely* let him take the wheel.

I came to realize, soon after this powerful epiphany that the secrecy and self-judgement I had for so long felt surrounding my sexuality had been incremental in my arrival to cancer's front door like this. That living in secrecy for so long had kept me tethered to living a half-life; one of limitation and fear and resentment of my own inner truth. Though, these emotions and all the turmoil they had wrought were also incremental in bringing me to this uncovering of my deeper life purpose, so I was grateful for them, for that.

However, it does need to be said that cancer is something we create. Something we manifest. Something that stirs inside of us, convincing our cells they are not worthy of health and vitality. That there is perhaps something deeply wrong with them; that they don't deserve to survive, much less thrive. And this description really aligns with the way I had felt for so long in regards to being gay. That perhaps I alone did not deserve real love and to truly be myself, because I was unusual - or felt as much on the inside, and had for the majority of my life.

I am convinced my cancer was formed from all the secrecy; the hiding of parts of myself. From my lack of self-worth, and the resentment that filled me up from having to live most of my life as less than my full and true self. And now that this truth has been burst wide open for me, I see clearly how others are moving in the same cycle. For it is a cycle, and one we absolutely must break.

I once heard someone speak about how cancer is created from deep, long-held resentment that convinces your cells they are not worthy, or causes them to adapt in abnormal ways. Resentment is a sense of sour indignation formed from being treated unfairly. Well, I had treated myself unfairly my whole life, in anticipation of the world doing so unto me, just as I had so often witnessed from the communities I had lived within growing up. I cut myself off from fully expressing my truth, in fear of being not only criticized by the world, but outcast from it, and from all the other beautiful things I loved.

I resented the fact that I'd had to hide part of myself out of fear. I felt guilt and shame around my sexual identity and the dissonance it had created in my life. I had criticized my actions subconsciously for so long, they had become a secret I never thought I could relinquish.

But I knew now that, no matter what my honesty brought my way, I absolutely had to learn to love myself exactly as I truly am, and accept my choices, past and future, with grace. I knew that this was optimal for healing my cancer, as well as my sexual identity.

I had inherited the idea that something was wrong with me for being gay. That something should be wrong with me for feeling the things I did; for feeling how I do! But this was just something I had been convinced of by others, and by the stories I'd heard about gays being chastised by society for their choices. In truth, I came to see that these perspectives on sexuality were nothing more than limiting beliefs that had been perpetrated out of fear and shame. Nothing more. And I did not have to subscribe to them! All that was necessary was to disown these feelings of inadequacy, and recognize that they were not my own, and did not have to designate my decisions.

This revelation has healed me. Through a ton of hard work and time spent discerning the differences between what was mine and what was not, I came to see this truth, and it freed me. I am grateful - beyond grateful - to God for this revelation, and all of the miracles it has brought me.

I am good enough. I am *worthy* of God's love. **Just as I am.** I know that now with every cell of my body. I am of God, and God is love. Thus I, too, am love, and my sexual identity does not affect that truth.

These fear-based mindsets had gotten lodged in my system, manifesting cancer. I may have felt lost amidst the confusion of it all, but only until I relinquished control, and replaced the fear with love. I chose loving, forgiving, and trusting thoughts to replace the negative patterns that had led me to where I was, living in lies.

A *whole lot* happened with me, to me and around me for me to get to this place, where I am today. I can now openly acknowledge and communicate my authentic self to the world. I don't believe that who we are is by mistake or happenstance. Every time I reflect on my life today and where I have come from, it gives me chills. Everything - every struggle, every "mistake", happens for a reason. Every trial makes us stronger, and more ready to share our learned lessons with the rest of the world.

I truly believe we are called here to heal - to heal ourselves, to heal each other, and to heal the world. I am finally, after so much struggle, recognizing the gifts *I received from that struggle*, and am ready to share my story to help others grow into their own self-love and confidence for being so organically unique as they already, naturally, are.

Since the beginning of my call into the ministry, I have been committed to my gift of preaching, pastoring, teaching and loving all of God's people. After all, that's what we as pastors are supposed to do when called into the ministry. Ministry simply means *to serve*. And I love serving God, and being connected to the Creator's creation.

I clearly remember, however, my initial resistance to accepting my call into the ministry. I did not want to be held to such a high standard. What with the intense pressure ministers are under to live a moral life, blameless of any conduct, *not* becoming a minister felt like a great idea. I did not originally want to do it. There were things going on in my life that were "not of God", meaning sinful. Sinful, meaning something clearly communicated in the bible that you should not be doing, yet you were doing anyway. And boy, was I doing it.

Doing it, doing it, doing it… was what I was doing on a regular basis. That is, sex with men, and with women, and often. **How** could I be a preacher, when I was not married and having all this sex? This was with consenting adults, all of whom were also Christians in the church. Men and women. But quite honestly, more men than women.

Women had always seemed more difficult than men. More was required by women than men, because of how they were culturized. With women, if I had sex with them, the threat was they could get pregnant and I would have to marry them. But with men there was no threat, except getting caught. And over the years, out of this fear, I had *mastered* not getting caught.

I have had many years of practice in not getting caught having sex with men. In my day, most of the time when you had sex with a woman, there was always someone you could tell about it and not get judged. But if you had sex with a man, you'd better not tell a soul. It was a secret you kept to yourself. A secret that was only acknowledged between you and the guy you'd had sex with. If the other person was not comfortable with the experience, you could not acknowledge this with them. You just sort of, had sex, without any pre or post conversations. These encounters, because of their secretive nature, weren't capable of allowing for any true intimacy.

I remember, with this one guy in my neighborhood, we called it "playing cards":

It all started this one night, while I was babysitting for a neighbor about four houses down from where I lived at the time. We were playing the game *Tonk* and he suggested that every time one of us lost we had to take off one piece of clothing. After several hands, we were both down to our underwear. I remember it was rather scary, but in a good way. After observing we were now in our underwear, he insisted on us going upstairs to this vacant room to try something.

I was following his lead, and the journey was getting more and more interesting. My heart was racing because I knew this was risky, but it also had the capacity to have a good ending. We took off our underwear, he got on top of me, and we did this thing called hunching. It was a happy ending. We went back downstairs, put our clothes back on, and he left... and I fell asleep on the sofa until the parents came home. So every time we wanted to have sex from there on out, we would just say to each other, *You want to play cards?* We both knew what it meant. It was our big secret, hidden from the rest of the world.

I have had many years of hiding and keeping my other self a secret. As a matter of fact, I have never told anyone about the cards before writing it down now. This is the first time I have ever disclosed this story. The secrets and the secret of my bisexual nature would continue for forty plus more years of my life.

I have been a pastor, a married man, a father, a spiritual leader and a sex addict for most of my adult life. I know that there are a whole lot of people who would love to dispute that I was not a pastor, and certainly *could not have been* a spiritual leader... and perhaps add that my marriage was also a joke. But this was my life, full of great successes and great failures. **This is my story** and the reality of it is that each and every moment of it has made me the man I am today.

I was affirmed by my successes and motivated by my failures to keep reaching for a higher quality of life. That higher quality of life meant that I did not have to live a double life. Did not have to live in lies, and could experience true freedom, as I believed God wanted me to have.

Resistance is the first step to change. And once I stopped resisting my call to the church, I found my life waiting for me to live it! I found how much I truly loved and reveled in it, and recognized that no path out there is ever straight and narrow. Every path we choose is wrought with the confusion to create questions we must then put in the work to answer.

For so, so many years, I lived my life with this sense of being unfulfilled. Sort of like an incomplete happiness. Like I was not ever quite fully happy. Always having to live with some kind of regret. Alongside which came chronic anxiety, and the fear of being found out. It was not right to be married to a woman while having affairs with men. But then it was also not fulfilling to like men but also like women.

Back in the late sixties and seventies, it was to me a sin to have sex, period, if you were not married. And then, it was a double sin if you had sex with men, I learned as I grew: To have sexual relations with men was worse than having sexual relations with women. At least if you had sex with a woman it was socially acceptable, but to engage with men was not so. So for many years, I lived with this conflict in mind.

In my spirit, I had to war often with being wrong in the choices I made around my sexuality. As far back as I can remember, even in my adolescent years, I had experiences sexually with men **and** women. Of course, back then it was boys and girls - more boys than girls - but they both were equally pleasurable.

Having encounters with guys was always easier for me, and a lot less complicated. We just did what we did, and walked away without any attached strings or obligations. But the girls were not always so easy - there were always demands and obligations with commitments.

With men, I could engage in a pleasurable moment, and then walk away. If we did anything ever again it was ok, but if not it was still ok. That's what made it so easy. Even though in my adolescence and teenage years, it was wrong to have sex period as I was under age, there was still this guilt that accompanied my feelings. Guilt that told me I was wrong doing it.

I simply followed my desires and rationalized in my mind that if I just ask God to forgive me and hopefully not do it again, it was no big deal. This was the cycle I repeated over and over again for most of my life. Trying not to have sex, but inevitably always engaging in sex with both men and women.

Now that I am free from the guilt and shame of living a promiscuous life, I am not free from facing the guilt of having destroyed or severely interrupted the lives of so many people - especially my family: My children and my ex-wife. I am happy to be openly gay and living my sexuality out loud, but there is still this nagging feeling inside me of having disappointed so many people who thought I was something different than what I had portrayed myself to be.

Knowing what I know today, I certainly wish it was a different world than the one I grew up in. In the world I grew up in, it was not safe nor acceptable to admit you were bisexual. To be accepted is an intricate part of human development. In Maslow's Hierarchy of Needs, belonging is the second-most important need of human support. We all want to belong, and when that's threatened, we do what we can to protect that sense of belonging - even if it means deceiving others to remain in their good graces.

I wanted to belong in my family of origin, and in my community of choice, and to expose my true self, somehow in my mind, threatened my place of belonging. I know many of you who read this will not want to admit to yourselves that when a person feels threatened they result to doing whatever it takes to remain safe. But it's true. We all do. We do what we can; we do whatever it takes.

The message I interpreted from the world was that **it was not safe to be gay**. Of course, that same message permeates our society today and is especially true in societies where gay people are killed and placed in prison for same-sex love. But we don't even have to take it that far. Right here in America, in certain circles, it is still life-threatening when someone is same-gender loving. *Safety* is another basic need in human development.

I have had a myriad of challenges and so far have survived them all. I am married to my partner of thirteen years. We got married in December of 2017. I was married to a woman; the marriage with her lasted for twenty-eight years. I came out to my wife twelve years into the marriage, and we stayed together sixteen years after. During that time, I lived as a bisexual man.

I hope for my story to change the world. But truly, I am simply happy to still be here, and to share it with you! My epiphany saw to that.

TWO

HOW CANCER BROUGHT ME
TO A NEW AWARENESS

I was fifty-three years old. It was January of 2006. Three years before

finding out I was in stage four of cancer; three years before my epiphany. And there I was, freshly diagnosed with Hodgkin's Lymphoma. I had started chemo treatments immediately, in February of 2006, and by November of that same year, I had gotten my last dosage of chemo.

And when I did a PET scan in December that year, the doctor came back and said to me, "We're going to monitor you. We didn't get it all." There was still just a tiny bit of the cancer cells left in my lymph nodes.

Mind you, when they first discovered the cancer, it was a very small amount; very treatable. As a matter of fact, the doctor had initially said to me, "95% of the people we treat for this kind of cancer are cured."

But when they were finished with my chemotherapy by that December, they had not gotten it all, and yet I just could not do anymore. I mean, the chemo, it just, was more than I could stand. And so, the doctor said to me that they were not going to do any more chemo, but that they were going to monitor me through PET scans I would have to come in for every six months.

And so that's what I did. I went in and out of the doctor's office every six months for PET scans.

My situation was still the same after the first six months. Then, I went back another six months later, and things were still basically the same. And on we went. But by the spring of 2009, they had noticed that the cancer cells had come back, as the doctor said, *with a vengeance*. And by September of 2009, I was in that fourth stage.

The epiphany of my life purpose actually arrived to me in a slow, steeping process throughout those three previous years. I dunno, maybe I'm a poor listener. But perhaps it just takes as long as it takes for us to realize our lessons; to see through the confusion pain brings, into the true heart of the matter. Whatever the reason, by 2009, when I recognized that it was fourth-stage - and the doctor said there was no fifth stage, and that if they didn't do anything at that point, it was going to be difficult for me to survive this cancer - I was ready to fight for my life, and win, no matter the cost.

My newfound purpose inspired me, and motivated me to do whatever it took to heal my body: So that I could be a voice for the voiceless. By the latter part of September, 2009, I had admitted myself to MD Anderson Hospital in Houston, Texas, to get ready for the stem cell transplant with a week of chemotherapy - a really, really extreme dosage of chemotherapy.

When I got back from the MD Anderson Hospital a week later, I went to see my oncologist in Atlanta for a follow-up checkup, as I'd been all the way out in Houston for the preparatory chemotherapy. Since I was living in Atlanta at the time – where my oncologist was, at Emory - I went there for my checkup. When I received my results, they informed me that my liver was practically non-existent. That's it: No more liver.

It was non-functioning. On the brink of absolute failure; on the verge of crisis. They sent me immediately to see a specialist, and when I went in, I was told that I could not do any more chemo. That my body wouldn't be able to handle it.

Now, mind you, I was supposed to get four of the rounds of chemotherapy I'd just gone through in Texas, in order to prepare my body fully for the stem cell transplant. The plan was, originally, for me to go back to MD Anderson Hospital every 23 days to get more chemo, so that after the four rounds, I would be ready for my stem cell transplant. But I did only the one round, and the one round was so severe - the chemo so strong - it just shut my liver down.

The specialist I'd gone to see, a gastroenterologist, said to me, "If we do more chemo, it is going to kill you."

Great, yes, I'd figured as much, I thought to myself, starting to get used to the sounds of bad news.

And then he said to me, "But then, you're in the fourth stage cancer, so one of these things is going to take you out: You do the chemo, you're going to die, or you don't do the chemo and the cancer is going to kill you."

I accepted the death sentence as best I could, and they put me on a medicine to get my liver back to a functioning level, and planned to monitor it closely. The specialist said, "If we can get your liver back to functioning healthily, then you can go back to your chemo, and get back on course for the stem cell therapy."

Somehow or another, I found my way into the office of a holistic doctor in Atlanta about two weeks later, who told me it was in my best interests to be on a strict regimen of eating healthily: No pork, no beef, no white rice, no white bread, no bleached foods; only eating really healthy greens and beans, and things like that.

He also put me on this regimen to alkaline my body, which included pau d'arco and French green clay, although the clay is grayer in color than it is green.

The holistic doctor told me, "Every day, I need you to put a teaspoon of this French green clay in a glass, and put about three to four ounces of water in with it. Then cover it up, let it sit overnight, and in the morning, put about 16 drops of the pau d'arco in the water and clay mixture, and drink it up. Every day."

Immediately after I left the holistic doctor, I went straight to a store here in Georgia that sells a lot of health food products, and got the pau d'arco and the clay. I started his suggested regimen right away, and kept it up through the winter months, never missing even one day; all the while eating only those things he had counseled.

I really had no issue with the holistic doctor's regimen. It was a hell of a lot easier to take than the chemo. Though it seemed almost too easy, I committed wholeheartedly to it, and did exactly as he had recommended.

Around the first of January, 2010, I went back to have yet another PET scan done to find out where the cancer was, and what my follow-up treatment was going to be to help support my failing liver and prepare for the stem cell therapy.

The results of the PET scan came back, and I remember it so clearly: The report from the PET scan said that my body was *completely* disease free. I've still got the paperwork today that says, just like this: "Your body is completely disease free."

The disease was nowhere in my body. For a heavy minute, I couldn't believe what it said. I thought, *What? No failing liver? No cancer? No stem cell replacement? My goodness... **no more chemo?!*** At first, I figured it was wrong somehow, while my mind ushered in a broad series of thoughts, such as, *they must have switched my results with someone else's; I'm sure they missed something; How can that even **be**???*

But no. It was *really*, actually gone! The doctors confirmed that there wasn't a trace of disease in my body. I mean, I go from a scan six months earlier saying that there was still tumor beyond tumor growing in my body, to being completely disease free?! I couldn't believe it. But actually, somewhere inside, *I kind of could.*

Now mind you, I had been dealing with this cancer since 2006. And even with these multiple, intense doses of chemo, it did not eradicate all of the cancer cells. Then, I got on this holistic regimen of pau d'arco and French green clay, with a supporting diet to alkalize my body, and the disease completely went away in a mere matter of months! Not to mention that my liver was functioning just fine, and then some.

You know, people often say, "You are what you eat", and I'm sure we all hear it and in our minds say, *Yeah, yeah sure…* but I'm still here; living proof that there may be more truth to that phrase than not!

I was just *overwhelmed* with emotion at those results. I felt as though a miracle had just graced my life! My hands were shaking with confused, grateful joy. Especially what with having been, at the time, in the fourth stage of cancer, I felt as though, *Okay then, that's it. God has clearly given me a second chance.*

My epiphany suddenly had real-world proof. I had found the cure to my illness, had healed *completely* from something that multiple professionals had told me was going to kill me, and now here I was, with the rest of my life in front of me.

And just what was I going to do with it?

I decided, in that moment, to make an absolute promise to God: That I would indeed fulfil my purpose. That I would be, in every

way I could, an advocate in the fight for the **LGBTQ** equality and justice. **I would preach, speak, and do everything in my power to help people live their authentic lives and to be free; to own who they are. And my teaching and preaching would be where I labored it.**

For seven years after that, I lived completely cancer free. And I have been fulfilling my promise, to the absolute best of my ability.

I had one issue with possible prostate cancer seven years after that last PET scan, so I went to my holistic doctor who said to me, "Are you on your regiment?"

I said, "Well, no, I've gotten off of it over the years."

He said, "Well then, get back on your regiment!"

So I did, and my, even *that* went away.

Perhaps, there is some correlation between having an alkaline body - being on my diet - and being a direct channel for God to move through. Maybe it was my absolute surrender in combination with that, which healed me. My diet felt to me like a tribute to God - an offering - to use me as His vessel, eating only that which is natural and whole - even if one of them was a thick gray clay I had to swallow each day.

Whether or not this is true, and no matter what you believe - hey, maybe it was the whole foods that made me whole again! - the proof is irrefutable. I was dying, went on a diet and took some recommended herbs, and then I was healed. I had early prostate cancer, went back on the regiment, and once again was healed.

I know in my heart that coming out and standing fully in my truth had very much to do with finding the path, walking it confidently, and being guided towards healing. I think we are meant to be our true selves; I think we are meant to be whole, and to heal. Heck, you get a scratch, and your body gets right to work healing it! I think we really just need to listen to and follow our own inner north - no matter what the rest of the world says or does - and be right with ourselves, and then, perhaps we find our way, no matter how lost we've been or for how long.

And what's even more amazing to me is how the answer; the pathway back to wholeness and health was revealed to me so effortlessly. All I did was follow the guideposts, and listen to my own inner voice for what my body could and could not handle, and I found my way.

I find, I found my *destiny*.

THREE

A CHILDHOOD ROUGH AS SANDPAPER

M y childhood was… an interesting one. There was the good, but there was also the bad and the ugly, and plenty of them to go around. Of course, the times combined have turned me into the man I am today, so I'm grateful for each element's role in my growth. And yet, it has been a struggle to shift my perspectives, in retrospect, to see clearly what my childhood was and what it was not. How it prepared me for adulthood, and how it damaged me.

I was no choir boy, nor did I have the perfect family growing up as a child.

I *am* grateful I had a roof over my head, food to eat, and wasn't denied any of life's necessities, as so many young LGBTQ folks are each day. Gay youth and homelessness appear to move hand in hand through time, where, as one progresses forward, so too the other.

The National Coalition for the Homeless put out a report from the Williams Institute that somewhere around forty percent of the homeless youth served by agencies identify as LGBT. And that the reason why so many young people are homeless is because they are rejected by their parents; they're rejected by their families.

Most of those youth who are out on the street and homeless have been left there, with nowhere to go, because of their sexual orientation and/or because their families do not accept them as such. As example, I remember one of the members of my congregation coming up to talk to me this one Sunday after church; a father who had said he discovered that his daughter was gay and that he needed to know what to do about it.

I looked at him with this puzzled look on my face, as he said frankly, "My biological daughter is gay, and I need to know what to do about it."

I said, with as much compassion and as little indignation as I could muster, "First of all, you love her."

He said to me, "Well, I don't know if I need to put her out, or try to help her see a therapist, or a psychologist, or something of that nature…"

I didn't know anything else to say, having been somewhat surprised by his mannerisms, except for: "No, you don't have to do any of that. All you have to do is love and support her."

All the while, I'm thinking to myself, *I have a gay son.... I love my son! How in the world would you even raise the question of 'what to do with her'? As though she were some disposable option. How do you question the love for your child based solely upon their sexual orientation?*

Now, I wasn't necessarily "out" as a child, but from what you may see in my story, clearly there was something there all along. Some truth to be exposed, which I worked to keep secret, all through my years, up into adulthood Something that had originated when I was first a child. Or was just always there, really; a part of who I am as an individual through and through, that took time to be revealed, and couldn't be welcomed in the midst of trauma.

It was in my childhood that I first encountered sexual abuse, and in my childhood where I first developed a low sense of self-esteem. Only, I had no idea I even had low self-esteem; not until I was fifty-six years old, and for the first time questioning the events in my life that led me to have cancer.

Shame was one of them, no doubt. And in order for me to reveal the truths behind the connections I've come to recognize between shame and cancer, I will have to get uncomfortable. I will have to expose the bad and the ugly moments from my life - at least, the pertinent ones - even though it is clearly not within my nature to do so; secrecy being one of my most enduring traits from childhood.

Yes, in order for you to get the full picture of who I am today, and see clearly the journey of how I healed myself into wholeness, I won't only telltale the joys and happy moments, but also the hardships, disappointments, pain and hurt that prevailed at times.

Most of what I experienced growing up felt normal to me, as it was what happened in most of the households in my family and neighborhood, as far as I could tell. Certain times were generally filled with great joy; such as holidays, where we would connect with both my mother's and father's sides of the family, all collecting together to share in the joys of celebration.

Both mom's and dad's families lived within walking distance, so it was never very difficult for us to all get together… nor to eat and drink while gathered. For food was a quality staple in the Meredith line, and honestly, there wasn't a Meredith who *couldn't* cook like a master chef!

Laughter rang through our home on the big holidays. The loudest laughter. The best food. These were the golden threads of my youth. I felt that the best cooks in the world brought their food under my parents' roof just for me to eat on holidays. And I'm pretty sure my childhood assumptions were spot on. My eyes like disks, I don't even think I'd have noticed any small family quarrels so long as they were happening around the time food was served.

I had the privilege of growing up with both sets of grandparents, and all of whom could cook a mean meal. Our family table was filled to the brim, and this is definitely another one of those traits I've carried with me into my adult years. Even now, one of my most favorite things to do is eat good food. I will go out of my way to consume something

40

tasty; traveling miles and miles to get a good meal under my belt... for, to me, eating is one of the most foundational, enjoyable activities I knew as a child!

In fact, I was always such a good eater that my grandmother's brother-in-law - my Uncle West - used to call me "The Eaten King" at every meal. I'd be set up at the end of the table, fork in one hand, knife in the other, a plate piled high with the most delicious-looking fare, perhaps I was drooling, I can't remember, and then Uncle West would look over at me smiling wide, shaking his head as he announced to the crowd, "The Eaten King is Ready... I think we'd better dig in!" And then I'd go to town.

Eating good food was one of the great joys of growing up as a Meredith. At family dinners, the older generations would stare in awe at my brothers and I going to town. They'd express from all sides of the room how impressed they were at how much we could devour in one sitting, exclaiming time and time again, "Where does it all go?" and laughing in harmony at their own wit. In fact, it was the core topic of discussion for the majority of the dinner hour, which would always end with someone asking my father the same question, "How on earth do you feed these boys?"

Along with the dependably delicious meal, came the constant flow of drinks. Though us youngsters weren't allowed to partake, the cupeth runneth over for our folks and theirs. Us kids referred to their alcohols as, 'the usual brown stuff, the clear stuff, wine, and plenty of beer', only knowing that when their glasses had one or the other, things were sure to get louder and louder as the night progressed.

Somebody would always, without fail, end up drinking too much, and that's when the ugliness would come out to play. If my father happened to be the one who'd drank too much, I would become instantly frightened. For, when dad drank, there was a particularly terrible kind of ugliness that would emerge. For some reason inside himself, he would always become violent, and very angry... most especially towards my mother, then directing it all her way.

I could never understand why my parents had such terrible, horrible fights every time my father drank. I just didn't understand why he got so angry. Especially at a party, with such good food and laughter, I didn't understand what there was to be angry about!

Not until I was much older did I realize that both of my parents possessed some really serious anger issues. Whenever they would argue, my father would plead with my mother to 'back off' and 'let him alone'. I remember thinking to myself during these arguments, *Mom, you need to stop cursing and screaming at him or he's going to blow up and this is going to get real ugly*, but mom would never stop before the argument turned into a fight... and then into a head-to-head battle.

And that's where my fear of dad's drinking came from, because after the argument became a full-blown battle, my mother and father would physically fight one another, until, as always, my mother ended up in the losing seat at the end, anger and sadness battling themselves in her watery eyes.

Those days were absolutely horrifying. I lost count long ago of how many nights I had gone to bed crying because of my parents' fighting. I mean, these were no small tiffs; they were all-out messy, and very, very traumatic and traumatizing to myself and my brothers. And even still, those nights weren't even the half of it, when it came to Dad's drinking.

Growing up, my Uncle West - the one who always called me 'The Eaten King' at family parties - owned a Gulf service station, where I happened to have my first job at thirteen. My father managed the gas station in the evenings to make extra money for the family. My father's regular job, however, was working in Foundry; casting parts for machinery.

While I am sure the extra money from working the gas station helped our family, it didn't feel like good thing, as my father would be gone from home so much. The other thing was, working at the station provided him the opportunity to connect with his vices: Drinking, as well as contact with other women. He cheated on my mother often.

The service station gave him the opportunity to flirt and engage in different affairs. The station wasn't the only place he could engage in his affairs, though; as he made his way to the bars every Friday and Saturday night - more often than not, coming home drunk. There were several occasions where he had gotten drunk enough to wreck our family car.

One incident I clearly recall was on a Friday night, after I had just gotten my driver's license. I went to the gas station where my dad was working, to swap vehicles with him, as my brother and I were planning to take the car out that night to attend our high school's basketball game. At the time, I had a 1954 Ford my grandfather had given to me. My father, on the other hand, had recently purchased a beautiful 1967 Grand Prix Pontiac convertible: Midnight blue with a light blue rag top. Clearly, I preferred to drive one over the other.

I was reluctant to ask my father about driving his new convertible; especially since I was a novice driver. When I got to the service station, it was clear that he'd been drinking, and his judgment was a bit off. Yet, to my surprise, he was in a generous mood! After a short lecture on how to drive, he willingly handed me the keys and - since it was a warm, spring night - insisted that I also let the top down.

My brother Greg and I left the gas station and… well, let's just say you couldn't have told me I was *not* the coolest teenager in Toledo, Ohio that night. My head was in the clouds. I could barely keep my ego intact, as I drove up to the ball game in this shiny, new convertible, where all my friends could see me.

The added feature of the evening was after the game, when everyone would always go to the Golden Arches on Monroe street. Of course, it was only a McDonald's, but back then we called it the *Golden Arches,* because of the yellow arches on each side of the restaurant - their signature look.

When we pulled up to the McDonald's that night, it was already full to the brim with teenagers from several of the neighboring high schools. Teenagers were known to converge on this place every Friday night during game season, so no one gave us a hard time for jamming the parking lot full of cars, and probably bringing the place past capacity.

When I pulled into the parking lot, all eyes were on us. We were the envy of everyone. The girls all wanted a ride in the car; the guys were jealous. It was one of the happiest moments of my high school career!

To add to the glory of the evening, after working my way through the crowd to order food at the counter for my brother and I, the young girl standing behind the counter waiting to take my order - I happened to know - had a crush on me. I had a crush on her too, but we were not dating at the time. [Although, we did get together later on.]

She only charged me for one order of fries, and smiled at me as she bagged up my order, heaping a bunch of extra food into the bag. I remember asking her what time she got off work, as I was hoping to show her my car-of-the-night, to score some extra brownie points. Unfortunately, I had to be back with the car by a curfew that kept me from being able to do so.

My brother and I had a ball that evening, and milked every second of driving around in that fine automobile. We stayed out until the very last stroke of our 10:30 PM curfew. When we returned, I backed the car into the driveway, as was the family custom.

I went into the house to see my mother sitting on the sofa, crying. My heart dropped, and I instantly presumed she and my father had been fighting again. This time, that wasn't the case.

I could hear my father sound asleep, snoring in the next room. When he snored, the house shook. Ignoring his rumbles as I always did, I homed in on my mother, and asked her why she was crying.

My brother and I sat down near her and listed as she told us between sobs, "Your father. Got drunk. Again [sob, sniffle]. He hit *seven* cars!"

Apparently, my dad had hit seven parked cars on his way home from his shift at the service station. Or more likely, on his way home from getting a drink at the bar after being drunk already at the station.

I thought about this for a moment. I'd passed the car in the driveway, parked just fine. Somehow, my father had managed to park the 54 Ford (thankfully, I had taken the better car out that night) in front of the house just fine. That didn't seem right.

My mother interrupted my thoughts with an answer to them, however: "He came in. Passed out in bed. Then some of the neighbor kids came by. Told me a mob of men were asking who the wrecked 54 Ford on the street b'longed to. I moved it. To the garage." She was becoming calmer as she continued to tell the story. "The kids. Were playing outside, and - and told the men they didn't know whose car it was. Thank *God!* Can you imagine what... what could have... *happened?!*" The last word was mouthed. She cried a bit more at the thought of it all.

According to my mother's account of the evening, she was afraid for my father's life; worried that someone would have seriously been hurt or killed, had the mob come into contact with my father. Mom feared the mob, sure. I feared for them, however, as pops was quite the strong, angry drunk.

After listening in distress to my mother's story of what had happened while I was out enjoying my evening in the shiny new convertible, I became curious to get a look at the Ford hidden in the garage. I took a walk outside with my brother, and was astonished. I could not figure out how my mother - much less, my father - could have driven the car:

46

The axle was broken; the front end completely smashed in. I stood there looking at what I considered to be *my* car, baffled by the loss.

On top of which, one of the angry men from the mob had written down the license plate number on the Ford, and reported that it had been in a hit-and-run. The police caught up to my dad the next day, and issued him several tickets and fines. My father ended up having to pay out a great deal of money to the owners of the other cars he had wrecked, completely negating the reason why he'd been working all those extra shifts at the service station in the first place!

This was just one of the many incidents revolving around my father's drinking problem; including, but not limited to several other car and motorcycle accidents, many of which were nearly life threatening. By some miracle; however, Dad always got away with just some minor scrapes and bruises. Again, another aspect to his drunken state that had always frightened me.

FOUR

FIGHTING AND SCREAMING

There was this one night, when the cops were called on Dad for domestic violence. The police came to our house to arrest him, just as my mother had called and asked them to, after he threw a knife at her. It just so happened that my mother had ducked, just as the knife went over her head.

Can you imagine, as a child, not only seeing your father arrested for trying to hurt your mother, but actually witnessing the potentially life-threatening event where Dad attacks and tries to kill Mom? It was horrible. Insane and horrible.

This one Thanksgiving dinner, not even the delicious food was able to distract me from the turmoil of the scene my parents had performed the night before. Late in the evening, my father walked in, completely trashed. Mom had been up late prepping the food for the next day - the usual turkey and dressing, greens and desserts - when all of a sudden, us kids were awoken by a crash and the sound of our parents' voices in rapid succession. It was clear they were arguing.

We lived in a three-bedroom, one-bath house. My brothers and I slept in the bedroom just next door to our parents', and thus we were able to pretty much hear everything. Somehow, their voices had traveled from the kitchen into their bedroom, getting only louder with every minute, until at some point, their voices dropped out, and they were silent, save for some grunts and groans. The rumbling was how we knew they were physically fighting. If only, they had been the type to fall into bed groaning, instead of on top of one another with malicious intent! I would so have preferred being grossed out and annoyed and embarrassed, than scared to death as I was.

As I lay in bed, tears streaming from my eyes down my cheeks, I resigned myself to stare up at the ceiling until I figured out what to do. What I should do… what I could I do, little man that I was. Really, only a child, completely terrified but growing numb from the repetition, knowing only the fears but grasping desperately for the hope.

I figured, had I attempted to intervene, that if Dad was willing to strike my mother so hard when he was so drunk, that he'd have no problem going harder on me for defending - or attempting to defend - her. I couldn't imagine what he'd do to me, but I knew I wasn't nearly his favorite of the family. I figured myself pretty low on the totem from how he treated me on the regular, and thought he might just not miss me as much as the others.

When I heard my mother scream from the other room, however; I immediately jumped out of bed without a second's thought, as too did my oldest brother, and together we ran out our door and through the hall to our parents' room next door. What we found was my father on top of my mother, apparently attempting to restrain her from trying to detain him. He wanted to leave, and go back out to drink again, but she insisted he would not be leaving the house the night before Thanksgiving, and that he was far too drunk for it to be a safe idea, anyway.

Mom asked my brothers and me if we could help her keep Dad from leaving. Screamed the command at us, more like… but I was far too horrified by my drunk father to be even close to capable of confronting him in any way, so I just stood there, frozen beside my mother, and verbally pleaded and cried at him to stop restraining my mother and to get off of her. My oldest brother, however, at my mother's command, jumped in between them and tried to push dad off of mom. Of course, his young strength was absolutely no match to this Korean War Veteran. Dad threw him off without a sweat - he was especially strong when drunk - while, at the same time, continuing to hold my mother down against the floorboards.

All I could do was cry. Mom screamed at me to call my dad's parents immediately, to tell them to come over to our house to stop my dad from leaving, and to tell them it was because he was too drunk to drive. By this point, my father had been the causing factor of many a car crash due to his being under the influence of alcohol, and extremely so. So naturally, his parents rushed right over to intervene.

My grandparents lived only four blocks away, so they were able to make it over pretty quick. By the time they got there, my father had exhausted my mother and us kids enough to break away and, as quickly as a drunk can, began to gather his things to leave. My father's parents immediately blocked his pathway, and spun my father around to sit him down next to where my mother had taken root. They took a good bit of time talking to my parents about the senselessness of fighting and arguing after that, while my father listened and responded attentively. Dad had the utmost respect for his parents, so he listened fine, but still insisted emphatically that he would be leaving to go out.

While my parents and my father's parents were still in the midst of their discussion, my mother's parents came into the house. They were so emotional, in angst to know what was going on, and then proceeded to pour their heart and soul out into trying to convince my parents of how dangerous all their fighting was. They pleaded with my parents to stop all the arguing and the fighting before someone was seriously hurt, or even killed. My ears ring with the memory of my grandfather - my mother's father - crying uncontrollably, grabbing his face and saying, "He's gonna kill my daughter!"

It was the wee hours of the morning by this point, the sun just peaking a wary eye over the horizon. My grandparents all left soon after, and the house settled itself into a kind of exhausted state of calm.

My father went wearily to bed, but my mother was still acting very strange. She wouldn't stop crying, and started walking down into the basement, all the while heaving heavy sobs. I didn't know what to do, how to calm her, or even if I should, so I just cried some more. A river of tears engulfed the whole of our house, and each one of our hearts, that night. When mom did reemerge from the basement, she sniffled her way into the bathroom, back out of the bathroom, and into our bedroom to tell us she "loved us so much but just couldn't take it anymore".

It was clear to us something was wrong with her.

Mom's swollen, sad eyes, hunched shoulders, hung head, and whole demeanor seemed alarmingly off. Where was the strong, determined woman who'd been raising me - fighting for me - this whole time? After all four of her children pleaded with her, asking what was wrong and what they could do, she sullenly spoke to us, saying how she was leaving, not just the house, but the whole world behind. She spoke softer and softer as she continued to tell us, trailing off at the end.

I didn't know what was happening to her. So I started running around, first the bedroom, then the hall, and eventually into the bathroom where I found an empty, open pill bottle spilled on the floor. My brother made sense of it quickly, and ran off to tell my father that she had taken a bottle of pills in an attempt to commit suicide. I was twelve. I had no idea how to handle this reveal; I knew only that my mother needed help, and that I didn't want her to go anywhere.

As soon as dad heard the news, he snapped into rescue-action mode. My mother had passed out on the floor soon after telling us she was leaving, so dad swooped down and picked her up - his strength coming in handy this time - and carried her to the car, closing her in the back seat, and taking off to rush her to the hospital. Before he left, he assured us that mom would be alright. As they drove away, I thought to myself what a horrible Thanksgiving this was, and continued to cry some more.

Later on the next day - Thanksgiving Day - my parents returned home. My mother was very lethargic, and so she swept right off to bed. My father filled us in, in her stead. Apparently, the pills my mother had taken weren't actually life-threatening, so the doctors merely pumped her stomach, gave her some meds, and sent her home.

By far, it was the worst Thanksgiving I'd ever had in my whole life, and one I've never truly forgotten. I couldn't even tell you if I ate that day, I was so down and depressed.

I wasn't feeling grateful for my family on Thanksgiving. I wasn't grateful for the home I lived in, the food I got to eat, or the sense of community that was usually so strong in our kitchen. Things had grown so tense between my parents, after years of the same struggle, that they would rather have left all us kids behind, than face one another and face their own internal struggles. I was frightened of the future, and how much worse it could potentially get; for, as far as I had witnessed from my parents all along growing up, things only got worse.

I know my low self-esteem stems from my mother's attempted suicide (even if she didn't actually threaten her life with the pills, she still *meant* to leave us). The sheer level of conflict between my parents directly contributed to my insecurities, between my mother's anger, and all that non-stop fighting in the house. I didn't feel I could trust my parents, trust my home, or trust myself. I didn't understand what I *could* trust, and what I could not.

I thought, perhaps, I could trust the church, and trust in God's divine grace, so I leaned into my experiences there after this, and leaned away from life at home. I started singing in the choir - yes, tried to become that good ole' choir boy - and formed relationships with several church members.

A few years after leaning into the church, and joining the choir, my uncle, who was a superintendent of the Sunday school at my church, asked me if I wished to attend the Congress with him. I was fifteen. The National Baptist Congress of Christian Education is a part of the National Baptist Convention containing the educational branch. A lot of young people - a lot of children - go there to take these classes, and then go back home to report to their churches on what they learned.

So, my uncle had chosen myself and this other young man, James Finney (now deceased), to go. Of course, my uncle has since passed away as well. But the three of us travelled together from Toledo to Miami, Florida for the conference, excited to learn and go someplace new.

After three days of the conference, my uncle Willie, my grandmother's brother, told me that there was a guy who wanted to see me, and speak with me. The gentleman had been the musician for the convention, and we had met briefly in the lobby of the hotel we were all staying in, earlier that afternoon. That night, then, my uncle told me to head over to that guy's room, and told me where it was and how to get there.

I had assumed that the purpose of going to this guy's room was to talk about participating in the music. I thought, because I sing in the choir, and he was the choir director and musician for the convention, that he had asked me up there to talk about some musical selection, or something to do with the music for the convention. My mind even touched on the possibility of some exciting, new opportunity through music or the church. So, I was going to his room to discuss that. Or so I thought.

When I got to his room, I knocked on the door, and the guy let me in. He was an extremely large guy, who looked as though he weighed 400 pounds.... I mean, he was huge. That in itself was intimidating, but especially so, since I probably weighed about 150 pounds, *if that*. I was real tall and skinny as a teenager. So, after inviting me in and closing the door behind me, this guy put the latch on the door, and locked it. I thought that was very strange, but I didn't think to say anything. It made me concerned, and the tiniest bit nervous, and left me thinking, *What's all this about, then*, but I didn't know to be suspicious. Not yet, at least.

The man told me to have a seat after bolting the door, so I did just that. I sat down on the hotel couch, but then he sat down really close next to me. He was clearly invading my space, but I was a young boy and suffered through. I was pretty used to being uncomfortable by this point, to be honest, and so I didn't move away or try to do anything, even though it was a bit much for me that he had sat so close.

He turned to look sideways beside me, took a breath, and said to me, "You know what I want you to do?"

I said in response, "No, I - uh - don't know. What do you want me to do?"

He said back, unchanged, "*You know* what I want you to do."

I said, "Uh. Excuse me? No, I do not know what you want me to do. What is it?"

And so he says - and I know this could sound a little vulgar, but he says - "I want you to screw me."

And I'm like, "Woah." I said, "I'm - I - I can't do that."

So he said, "I'll pay you."

And I was like, "Um, I - I - I -"

He said, "Listen. It will be okay. You will be fine. Just don't be nervous. Calm down. It'll be okay. You'll be fine."

And I'm like, "I - I can't do it."

I, at the time, just happened to have this little knife in my pocket. As I sat there, I remembered how I had gotten it earlier that day at this little shop James - the other young guy who had come along on the trip - and I had found and gone into. We each had bought a small pocketknife there, cause we thought they'd be cool as souvenirs. Sitting in the room with this 400 pound man, I felt lucky to have gone there, and so, thought to myself, *Well, I could pull this knife out, and scare this guy, or threaten him... but then, he's so large, what if he takes the knife from me, and does something to me?*

I thought for awhile about what to do, as this man just watched me with his mouth watering, waiting for me to succumb to his ills. I ended up being too scared to pull the knife on this guy, as I figured I would lose that fight, and that something much worse than what he was asking me to do could end up going down.

So, he, after watching me in all my anxiety try to make sense of what to do, said, "Well, here, just take off your clothes", and I said in return, "No, I'm not taking off my clothes."

I said so firmly, and yet he started to unbuckle and unzip my pants, pull them down, and then perform oral sex on me. I was a young teenage boy, so pretty much anything gave me an erection back then, and this was unfortunately no exception.

He took note of my erection, and then insisted that I penetrate him. I honestly tried to do what he'd asked, but couldn't maintain the erection. I was so nervous; so overwhelmed and mortified by the whole experience, that I, somewhat luckily, couldn't maintain the erection, and couldn't follow through with what he had wanted me to do.

No doubt, he did try to revive me and force the penetration for another twenty some odd minutes. But eventually, he did get frustrated enough to give up, saying to me, "Aw, just forget it", and telling me to leave. I remember him then reaching deep into his pants pocket, and pulling out twenty dollars, and telling me not to tell anybody about what had happened, as he slapped it into my palm.

I walked quickly back to my room, looking over my shoulder and trying to make sense of what had just happened. Interestingly enough, when I got back to James, it turned out he had had a similar experience. I filled him in - without all the gory details - on what had happened to me in the guy's room, and he said in horror, "The same thing happened to me!"

Apparently, my uncle was not such a great guy. Apparently, he had set up the rendezvous in the lobby of the hotel earlier that day, where we had initially met the older men he then sent us to meet with that evening. He invited us to this conference to usher us secretly into this undercover system of teenage molestation. So, I guess I was molested. And it wasn't damn near the last time it would happen to me. Apparently, it wasn't the first either.... only the most vivid.

You know, I didn't know anything about gay people back then. Homosexuality was an evasive element to my mind. Even though I'd had experiences with guys in my community, such as masturbating together, and stuff like that, I knew *nothing* on the same level as what this oaf of a man had now thrown my way with this experience. Any experiences I'd had before this one were just guys experimenting, or whatever you call it. Consensual and innocent in their exploration.

After this experience, I called my aunt, who was also there in Miami at the conference with us. I called and told her what had happened, and she said to me in return, "Oh no! Oh, Dennis.... I'm so sorry this has happened to you. I should've had this conversation with you to let you know that there are people out there like that, and to be careful!" She went on and on, but I couldn't believe she knew about it in the first place and could just accept it like that!

I mean, this was back in the sixties!

After I got off the phone with my aunt, I called my mother, and told her. My mother was very disappointed, and she said the same thing to me as my aunt. Then she went on further, saying, "Don't tell your father, cause your father would just travel to Miami and do something to this guy. He'd be devastated - beyond devastated. So let's just keep this between you and I."

So I never really told the story again after that. No one else ever knew.

Following that event, my uncle (who knew what he had done) would often do things to me. He would corner me, or find me, and molest me. He would perform oral sex most of the time. And then give me money to cover it up. He did this to me until he died, and I honestly can't really recall the age I was when it all ended.

These experiences ushered me into this phase of thinking it was my fault that it had happened. I spent years and years and years ping-ponging around, confused and easily triggered. I honestly didn't come to terms with understanding that I was molested until I was in my fifties! I was only fifteen at the time it all started, so I had just accepted it, figured something was wrong with me that I had been pushed into these experiences, figured I deserved it, and allowed it to happen... over, and over, and over again.

All those years, due to how I'd had experiences with guys in my neighborhood as I mentioned earlier, I had thought I was a willing participant in my uncle's advances. I thought it was a normal thing, that just felt a little weird, and so I continued to allow it to happen, never knowing to question things of a world I already didn't trust. I didn't really recognize that I was underage, or that I was molested. It never even dawned on me, that whole time.... Not until I was in my fifties, and my current partner, Lavar (who works in childcare), kept telling me, "You were molested. How do you not connect to that?"

Finally, with Lavar's [my partner of thirteen years, now] support, I was able to connect all the dots, and come to terms with the truth: that it was in fact inappropriate, and it was molestation. It was not consensual. I was molested.

I wish it hadn't happened, sure. Of course I do. But it did, there's no changing it, and it set me on a life of an absolute misplacement of trust when it came to sex. Mistrust became my norm. I was still a scared little child, only I was no longer a child, and was moving through the world as an adult with all this baggage I never even realized I was carrying around. It was like having a broken arm, only not realizing your arm is broken, accepting it as it is, and then going out in the world to work a job that requires the meticulous use of an arm that doesn't know it's even broken. It is only protecting itself. Self-preservation, and all that. Things hurt - a lot of things hurt about the entire ordeal - but I didn't know what to make of the pain at the time, or how to process the experience, and instead numbed it out, and hid it all away, like so many other things.

FIVE

GROWING UP IN THE CHURCH

Only now have I healed the wounds of my childhood. Only now, have I finally been capable of witnessing the holes in my wholeness; those places where I had been stunted and frozen in time.

There really was so much about my childhood - so many good times, and nurturing moments - that *did* actually support me in becoming whole. You know, it's really never *all* bad. Just, it can prove tricky to see the good when you're mostly living from a state of fear, confusion, and secrecy. When you're living mostly in your head, nervous and anxious for the future and what bad it might bring.

I spent a lot of my time trying to escape the places where I felt I had to brace myself in preparation for some painful experience that was bound to occur. For me, that place was the church.

The church did something for me that, growing up in my home, did not do. I want to make that distinction clear, as, for me, the church brought into my life a particular value - a purpose worth living - that I don't feel was there in my home growing up. It was to a point, but as you see from my story, there were a lot of fearful experiences around that overshadowed any good that came out of my home.

My home life was honestly okay, but the church was better. It did something great for me! The church took me out of my pain. The church helped me to escape the parts of my life I had wished weren't happening, and it gave me hope that those things I didn't understand would eventually come to light and I would be protected by God's love. It also granted me a sense of community, where people were decent, and they were there for the same reasons you were: to celebrate God's loving salvation. The church, for me, was just overall a really, really good experience. And I'm thankful I could find such a place of support to carry me through such difficult times.

I felt a bit less self-deprecating at church than I did when at home. As I mentioned before, I was far from my father's favorite, and I also feared him somewhat. This made it difficult for me to ever fully "calm down" or relax into my true self when I was at home; which, ironically, is the one place you hope to be able to do just that!

My oldest brother, Chucky, was always an extremely talented kid. He was so talented, and so intelligent, that he had even taught himself how to play the bass guitar, and at quite a young age! He was always so well loved and appreciated in the family. He was by far the favorite.... and on top of it all, was able to bond with my father over sports. He was an all-around athlete, playing football, baseball, and then some. Where I was far from it, my eldest brother was an absolute guy's guy - buff, tough, and physically focused, yet never taking himself too seriously, all the same.

Needless to say, my father adored him. You could see it; they had a special connection I was... unfortunately, jealous of. You see, I've got no talent whatsoever. Never did. Or at least, I didn't see myself as a generally talented individual. I was really clumsy, wasn't talented with any instruments, and couldn't play sports to save my life! Wasn't good at basketball, wasn't good at baseball, wasn't good at football... I mean, there was not one sport that I tried that I was actually decent at.

My oldest and youngest brothers, though, excelled at all of that. My younger brother, Gregory, was excellent at running track, and played football so well he was once invited to try out for the Denver Broncos! So them two were, of course, father's favorites! They sure were... he just loved that they were so inclined to be athletic, and as a result, had a different kind of relationship with them than he ever had with me.

Dad valued sports, and would spend his Sunday - every Sunday - watching football on the couch while talking to his friends and engaging in the season's drama. Whatever the season, there was athletic drama, and there was my dad. If it was baseball season, he was into baseball; if football season, he was into football... and so on. He just loved sports, and loved and understood others who did too.

I was living in this arena where, if you were a young boy, sports were the one thing to get you recognized. Since I was clumsy, and not at all athletic, however; I didn't really stand out socially, and especially not so with my father. It was as though I went unnoticed. As a boy, I of course took that to mean that I wasn't important, appreciated, or of any value. I could see, even back then, the value that was placed on my two athletic brothers for their abilities and talents, and could clearly see that because I had no talents as such, it was as though there was no value attached to my place in the home.

I connected much more deeply with my mother growing up, than I ever did my father. My mother did so many things with all of us children, and wasn't ever so distracted by work and other drama, that I felt she knew each one of us so well, and loved each one of us in a much more individualistic way than what my father seemed to feel was necessary.

My mother would take us kids fishing, to the zoo, or roller skating, and she taught us all so many things. She taught me, for instance, how to sew, how to cook, how to roller skate, and even how to dance! She was just the type of mom who made sure to spend a lot of quality time with her children.

She interacted with us in so many things that I never felt devalued by her nurture or attention. She seemed to spread herself quite evenly across each one of us four boys: Chucky, the eldest; then me; then Gregory, my younger brother; and finally Delta, the youngest among us. And although I did feel that perhaps my mother favored Gregory over the rest of us, I didn't mind it so much as I did with my father, as Mom truly did seem to love each of us deeply.

Still, though, I struggled to find my value in the home. Two brothers favored by the father, one brother favored by the mother... and then there I was. Alone in a repressed, gay limbo, just trying to find my way out.

I often played by myself, and I was often happier that way. With my brothers, there were always quarrels, and battles where we'd rival one another. It was exhausting. And sometimes the fights we had were pretty severe, leaving one or more of us youngsters with battle wounds.

One day when I was outside playing in the backyard by myself - no idea where my brothers happened to be at the time - when I spotted this scarf blowing in the street. I went and grabbed the scarf, and put it on my head.

When my mother saw what I'd done, she stepped out from inside the house and said to me, "Don't put that scarf on your head." Then went back into the house to go about her chores.

I didn't listen, since I didn't see why I couldn't - nay, why I shouldn't - play with the scarf if I really wanted to. So I continued to play with this scarf, when my mother came outside once again to tell me, "I told you to stop playing with that scarf. If I catch you playing with that scarf again, you're gonna get in trouble." And then she, once again, went back into the house.

Now, I'm guessing she had really just stepped inside the doorframe and out of sight to watch me and see if I would listen to her command because, sure enough, not one minute later had I started playing with that scarf again, attempting to tie it over my head, when she came barreling back outside, and this time with a vengeance.

Disciplinarian that she was, my mother ordered me into the house, and told me she was gonna whip me. She dragged me inside and pulled out her switch. Leaning my arms and face into the side wall, she proceeded to whip me, and whip me, and whip me and whip me.

Whenever my mother would punish us, it was as though she became possessed, going into this sort of wild, ravaged rage as she did so. In fact, my mother whipped me so severely over this whole scarf thing that I couldn't take it anymore, it hurt so bad, and so I started to run away from where she'd planted me against the wall. On my way away from her, however; I slammed into the back door of the house, hit my head, and wound up with a big old knot on my forehead in tribute to my attempt to escape my mother's brutality.

Once my father was home from work, he said hello to us all, and eventually wound up noticing the unavoidably large hickey knot on my forehead. He asked me what had happened, and so I explained to him… how mom was whipping me in a blind rage, and I tried to run away, but ran straight into the back door instead. When my mother confirmed it, my father became extremely angry with my mother, threatening her in saying that if she ever punished me that severely again, she would have to answer to him.

This was the one and only time, far as I can recall, when I really felt like, *Ah, my father loves me!* Where, normally, I honestly didn't feel like he did love me. He was gone all the time, hard-working man that he was, and when he was around, I was last on his list of where to disperse affection.

This here was the one and only time throughout my childhood and adolescent years, where I saw in my father that he truly cared for me. It was something I'd never seen before, and frankly didn't see again. I remember thinking with amazement, *Wow he cares!* So shocked as I was that he did in fact love me, and care.

Little boy though I was, his actions stood out strongly to me, stark in contrast to his original efforts. His standard operating procedure. I never forgot - could never forget - even though I didn't appreciate his threat of hurting my mother. Even though his threat wasn't something I wanted fulfilled, I felt grateful that my pains had not gone unnoticed for once, as they so generally were.

Hindsight giving the gifts it does, I do believe my mother so violently beat me that day out of a fear for what she saw in my actions. I believe she perhaps had already wondered whether something was different about me, didn't understand or know what to do with it, but was too scared for me to do nothing about it. I wonder if she saw me playing with a scarf, or saw something in my demeanor that was different from that of my brothers, enough so to perhaps even think specifically that I might be gay.

Back then, you know, boys did boy things. *And shouldn't be doing girl things like that.* So I wonder, and so too with Dad. Did he ignore me because he thought I might be gay? It's a bittersweet feeling to consider that those things you spend your lifetime trying to keep hidden and protect about yourself can be so transparent to those that know you. I feel a vulnerable kind of shudder in thinking that my parents may have understood something on a basic level about me when I was a young

69

boy, that I have only recently found a doorway to unlocking and revealing to myself.

Generally, growing up in that home, I felt like an outcast. I didn't really... fit, with the rest of my family. I never really saw a clear resemblance between myself and my brothers, nor between me and my father... and I didn't *really* resemble my mother very much, either. If anything, I did resemble my grandfather - my mother's father - more than anybody. And I really only feel this way because everybody in the family or close friends would always say to me, "boy, do you look just like your grandfather!" I always heard that, from everybody, but wasn't sure it was enough of a similarity to help me feel accepted and like "a part of the family". On top of which, my skin color is a bit lighter than the rest of my family members.

In so many ways, I didn't feel I fit in with my loved ones. I didn't feel assured of my place at their side, so I questioned it constantly, and was always on the lookout for external sources of validation.

One source of validation I was able to recognize came in the form of fashion! I know, I know... what a stereotype. But truly, ever since I was a young pup, I loved being fashionable. Presenting myself with flair. And this just so happened to be one area - really, the only area - in which my father and I could connect. Dad was always super fly and fashionable, to the nines! His generally handsome nature worked well in a good suit. And my mother, too, was very beautifully fashionable when she went out. Both my parents were exceptional dressers.

I used to absolutely *love* watching them get dressed up to go out on the town. While my brothers would all hold up in their rooms preparing for some free time away from the ever-present gaze of mom and dad's watchful eye, I would sit in the living room outside their room, on their bed, or wherever they would let me, and watch them doll themselves up.

Out of all my brothers, I took on this sort of fashionable persona. I am still, by far, the most fashionable of any of them. No doubt, but even back then, I was fascinated by self-adornment and looking good, and feeling clean and neat. It felt good to get dressed up like my parents, and so I really took to heart this interest in dressing well and being fashionable.

My father once said to me, "Oh, Dennis, you dress so well!" And it blew the socks straight outta my shoes. I couldn't believe it. He seemed *proud* of me, and for something I really loved! I was always putting the time in to take care of what I wore, choose carefully how I dressed myself, and was even the first of my brothers to learn how to tie a tie. Apparently, Dad had taken note! And then decided to applaud and affirm me for being so cognizant of how to dress and put colors together... affirm me in going the extra mile in being fashionable, which I was honestly doing because my parents were both so fashionable.

My favorite place to flaunt my fashion choices was at church. Though not so for my parents, I had always placed church high up on the totem pole of personal activities. Mother didn't really attend church during my childhood. And my father would go every now and then, maybe once or twice a year, but that was it.

Truly, my grandparents were the religious rock in my family, deeply steeped in the church and all its offerings and celebrations. My uncles on both sides of the family would show up to church more often than my parents, but even still with all that family there, I felt very supported and welcomed. As though every Sunday was the *best* Thanksgiving feast celebration I had ever had.

Many of my family members who did attend church regularly, and were quite active in the social events coordinated by the church, held various leadership roles and positions there. Very much so because of them, and because of their involvement, I felt recognized and validated at church; especially in contrast to how I felt at home. Church affirmed me, the church saw me, church made me feel important. The church I attended growing up, Cavalry Baptist Church, embraced me differently that I was embraced in my own home.

And perhaps, you know, that's perfectly normal! I dunno. Just, church made me feel important, and recognized. Basically, everywhere my home life failed to seemingly support me, the church supplied me with more than I needed.

Thus, I started singing in the choir and attended Sunday School, and did really everything I could that was offered, as a means of remaining active and around a system I felt I could depend on for support. And how did I do that? Mostly with the help of my grandparents.

Because of them, I felt like I had a place. Like I belonged there.

My grandparents would pick my brothers and me up from our house before church each Sunday. Or, at least, they would try to. We lived about six blocks away from the church, and whenever we weren't ready on time for my grandparents' pickup, would have to walk those six blocks straight down Vance St. to the church.

Of course, it felt like a long six blocks, you know, as we were children, so we did our best getting dressed in time for pickup. Only problem was, Grandma was an *avid* Sunday School Goer, absolutely religious and rigid in her attendance. She was quite insistent in her study of the bible, so she would spend the time first at school, then at service, devout in her attentiveness throughout.

My mother insisted, when we missed pickup, that we absolutely *had* to go to church (albeit a bit hypocritical of her to say), and that if we couldn't be ready on time, that we would heave to walk. Timely attendance for Sunday service wasn't optional. And if we didn't make it to church, we weren't allowed, by her, to do anything else for the rest of the day.

Luckily, I for one was highly motivated to attend church. The people loved me there! Always commenting on how well I was dressed, the older ladies pecking a kiss on my cheek or embracing me, the men fervently shaking my hand with a big smile of support. I felt so deeply affirmed for who I naturally was; so appreciated and connected to this sense of community there.

There was this one woman in the church, Miss McFarlane, who wrote plays to put on in church. She just *loved* her some Dennis Meredith, and so would always write a part for me. I starred in many a role, most often portraying a preacher, and the audience just loved me, eating up what I would dole out! I learned how to act in church! I became a little actor; I was a little star!

So, here I am: Completely unathletic, without affirmation in the home; yet, a natural performer, with absolute affirmation at church! I was able to come alive in church, and felt publicly affirmed and valued and appreciated. Most importantly, I felt like I fit in with the church community.

As a matter of fact, I became a lead singer, I became a choir director... I absolutely grew and evolved in the church. And eventually, it was where I became a preacher, and accepted my call to the ministry I mean, I just kind of grew up there. Grew into myself there. I became somebody, because of what the church did for me. It was absolutely instrumental in my life for helping me to develop who and what I am today. Now here, today, I'm a pastor, I'm a preacher, a singer and musician, and all of that started because of... well, because of the church! And because I made that connection where I felt safe to express myself fully and grow into my natural gifts.

What has proven interesting to me is that my oldest brother, Chucky, at one point was very much heavily involved in the church as well. And the people loved him, and he excelled, as he does in everything else in life. He excelled almost to the point where, in the church, he was overshadowing me; but, for some reason, he didn't have the same affection for church as I did. And so, he pulled away while I remained. My youngest brother, as well, is still quite active today, and found many of his own affirmations in the church as a child. But for me in particular, it really just shaped me, and my thinking about myself and about the world.

To top it off, my church was genuinely supportive. So many churches and religiously affiliated groups would bash gays back in those days, but not even a smidgeon of that kind of talk was tolerated at my church. As a matter of fact, there was a lot of gay people in the church. Not that I knew it at the time, or even really understood it at all, but I overheard subtle mention from time to time amongst the adults of the congregation about he or she being gay. Never with disdain; for, it was never an issue to the members of the congregation.

In all honesty, I'm unsure as to whether being gay was really an issue in my home growing up, as I had a cousin who was very openly, flamboyantly gay, and yet the entire family embraced him! Perhaps, then, my wonderings about my mother's beatings are off base. Perhaps she could accept the possibility to a point, but maybe just didn't want her son to experience the perceived societal hardship that came from such a choice. I'll never truly know for sure.

I am sure that there had to have been some subtle sociological inferences, references and messages that I internalized as a child about what it meant to be gay, but I just don't recall bashing of any kind from the pulpit or the members. I cannot even recall whether the pastor ever preached or touched on the topic of gayness as sin, as the classic tale is known to provoke.

The struggles I experienced with my sexual identification came into play for me as an adult, more than anything. As a pastor-preacher, working in the church, I have indeed been confronted with it. And have actually been able to use the confrontations I've experienced to help support and nurture other families in reckoning with a gay family member.

I've struggled from time to time, as an adult, wondering about this idea of lying with another man as sin, but luckily it wasn't a factor for me during those developing years. Of course, of course, it became an issue in regards to my experiences being molested, but even then, my worries were very confused and personal.

I simply didn't grow up with that old-school paradigm that everything was sin, including being gay. And I thank my church for that. For not filling my head with more garbage than was already being supplied in bulk from the rest of the world. For not forming within me a foundation of sinful guilt and fear and shame, the way I know so many churches did. And yes, the church did preach around the issue of premarital sex as a sin, but I didn't even grow up with any kind of - I don't know - teasing around these issues as a young pup.

As a matter of fact, even in my family space, my gay cousin was never given a hard time, and rather, was embraced and adored by the family for his differences. Sure they called him flamboyant, with a cheeky grin, and thought his way of life was a bit *far out* from how the members of my family generally viewed the world, but he was at least able to be freely himself, without any muck messing up the works.

I think because of this support I received from the church, and because I wasn't ever steeped in the sin-guilt of the common man, I am more capable of accepting and affirming with who I am today, and the message of my choices. Even though, as I grew up, I did struggle with this voice in my head telling me that "something was wrong with me", I didn't have the messages - or at least the sermons - in my head that reinforced the thought.

The sociological norms were what conditioned me most towards feeling like same sex attraction was wrong. But the church, nah. The church gifted me the forbearance to traverse my internal struggles with grace. The church gave me a place of value and significance and importance, and it fed into that part that says I belong.

Maslow's Hierarchy of Needs refers to the importance of belonging, and luckily, where I wasn't feeling so supported at home, the church provided me kinship, community and a kind of kindness I had never before known. It allowed me to continue along the journey to self-actualization, and find pride in my own natural uniqueness to contrast the fear of rejection I felt from home.

The church met my basic needs where my family could not. Did not. And thusly, I had an indelible connection with the church, because it met a significant need that helped me to develop as a person. As an individual.

I guess that's why I'm still in it today! Still so active that I've made a career out of being in church! Church wraps me in love. Envelops me in support and affirmation for who I am… for whomever I naturally express as.

SIX

THE MARRIAGE PART ONE: FALLING IN LOVE

In late December of 1976, I left Toledo and moved to Birmingham, Alabama, to take on a job as a television news photographer. I had previously worked in television news for a few years back in Toledo, Ohio, where I was born and raised. Then I heard about this job opening in Birmingham as a news photographer, so I sent my resume, and ended up getting the job.

A few weeks after I moved there, I decided to join Sardis Baptist Church. I quickly became a fairly active member of the church, and started singing in the choir, working with youth, and eventually serving as one of the lead soloists of the choir, as well as choir director.

I was participating pretty heavily, all the while making connections with other members of the congregation. This one day about eight months after my move, after a sufficiently devout Bible study, this beautiful young woman came up to me, and invited me over to her apartment for dinner. Her name was Lydia.

Lydia was a very active member of the church. She served as Sunday school teacher, sang in the choir, and participated in various other church events and such. Lydia and I knew each other somewhat before she asked me over for dinner. A spot of conversation here or there, whether after Bible study or during a rehearsal break during choir. Nonetheless, those interactions were simply through the church; whereas, she was inviting me over for something that felt ever so slightly more like the next level.

After she approached me and asked me over, being the gentleman I considered myself to be, I accepted the invitation with a kind smile, and made my way over to her apartment at the agreed upon time.

When it came time to eat, she brought out the food she had prepared. I'll never forget the flames of discomfort that hit my face as she put out the plates, and I saw her meal of choice: liver and onions. Blech! I absolutely hated liver and onions at the time. Nevertheless, my mother had instilled in me that when somebody else cooks for you, you must be courteous and eat what they've prepared and put before you. So I struggled to get down those liver and onions! Luckily, she had made peas and mashed potatoes, so at least I had something a bit more palatable to force it down with.

I might add that I'm a fan of liver and onions today, by the way. And that, to be honest, in retrospect, Lydia had made a *mean* liver and onions that night!

Though I decided not to share my distaste of the meal choice with Lydia, she and I had much to discuss. We talked pretty good all that evening. Eventually, in the latter hours of our small dinner soiree, Lydia brought up the topic of sex, asking me as casually as I figure she could muster, what my feelings were regarding premarital sex.

Well, I had just so happened to be casually dating another young woman during this time, and had thus brought with me no agenda nor romantic intentions that evening. Plus, I was *not* the type to handle two women at once. So, when Lydia asked me about sex, I attempted to kindly bow out of the entire conversation topic, making blabbering excuses as though I was not the type of person who would engage in premarital sex. Although, this was not, in fact, true.

I finished my dinner, and left as politely as I could, without much more conversation. After that, we had no contact outside of church cordialities and such.

March of 1978 I bought a motorcycle. I was in need of someone willing to give me a lift up to North Birmingham, so I could pick it up after purchase. One Saturday afternoon, I was ready to meet my new motor baby, but there wasn't anyone around who could give me a ride.

Lydia just so happened to play tennis on weekends at Birmingham Southern University, right across the street from where I lived at the time, so I thought it was worth a shot to see if she was there and could spare the time to help me out.

When I asked her if she could give me the lift, she dropped what she was doing, said, "Hey, sure, it's no problem" with a smile as she stretched out her shoulders, and then off we went in her car up to North Birmingham.

On the way there, I asked her if she'd ever ridden a bike before. She hadn't, so I asked her if she wanted to go for a ride with me. It was a gorgeous spring day in Birmingham, and I couldn't wait to hit the road on my new bike.

She said, "Yeah I would love to!"

After we got the bike, I followed her back to her place. She changed into some jeans, and she looked good. I was excited to get on that bike with her, so we did, and we rode and we rode and we rode.... As a matter of fact, we rode all day long that Saturday. We had an absolute blast! Just a wonderful time.

After a long day, I took her home, thanked her for not only helping me pick up my bike, but for spending the day with me, and told her how much fun I had had. Then, basically, I didn't contact her again. I just, didn't have anything else to say to her after that. And that was it. I never really saw that day as a date; rather, I had seen us as out together, as friends, having a good time. So I left it where it was.

Months later, Lydia again approached me, after church this time. She had purchased a new home, and then mentioned something about how

I work in TV. She asked me if I could come over and take a look at her TV, as something was wrong with it, though she didn't know what. I guess she figured, since I had worked in TV, that I somehow knew how they worked, too… but unfortunately, this wasn't true. Working in TV, you rarely actually touch one.

Anyways, I told her I would be happy to come over and take a look at it, where after she added the bonus of informing me that I could also see her new home, while I'm at it.

One afternoon shortly after our fairly short conversation, I made my way to her new house. She informed me upon my arrival that she was set to have a housewarming party at the end of the week, and needed the TV to be in working order by then. So I took a look, doing my best work to clear up the picture quality, all the while maintaining the illusion that I knew anything at all about how to actually repair a television. All the while, Lydia and I fell into another one of our *conversations*. We talked and we talked and we talked and we talked and we talked. I mean, we just went on and on.

After I did what I could with the TV, I said to her I would be leaving, and as I turned away from her to leave, she stopped me, saying, "Where you gotta go."

It wasn't so much a question, but I responded, saying, "Oh I have to wash my hair." (I still had hair back then! Sadly, there's no hair left to worry about washing, anymore.)

She responded, "Well, let me scratch your scalp for you."

Lydia had this blue lounge sofa set up in her living room. So I consented, made my way over, and sat on the floor with my back up against the lounge, while she straddled me. She wasn't really scratching my scalp so much as she was rubbing it, so I pretended like I had fallen asleep, to see where she was going with this whole thing. It seemed like one ruse led to the next that night; we simply volleyed them back and forth. Lydia was very good at tennis, after all, and I was good at secrets. We were perfect opponents.

At one point as I was pretending to sleep, Lydia bent down and kissed me on the forehead. I thought, *Ah. Now I get it.* I hadn't ever possessed a talent for reading women, so I really needed the come-on to be right in my face, in order for me to see it at all.

When she kissed me, I "woke up", turned around, and returned a kiss. After a minute's eye contact, we moved into this passionate moment of kissing. After a little while of that, we broke apart - before it went any further. We each muttered a reasoning to the other about getting up early for work the next day. The age-old adage! So, I turned, and this time, I left.

Lydia's housewarming party took place the following weekend. Her mother, sisters, and most of her extended family were in attendance amidst this house full of people. At some point, I was passing through the kitchen for snacks, when I overheard Lydia's mother say to her, "Lydia, that is one nice man!" She was really alluding to the idea, *Lydia, you need a husband and this man looks like a great candidate!*

I had no way of knowing whether she was referring to me or not, but because of the other night, I figured it a worthy guess. I took note of the comment, even though marriage was not even somewhat, remotely on my mind at the time, and I was still technically involved with this other woman. The relationship with this other woman whom I had been seeing was quite tumultuous, however; and provided much more conflict than comfort. I was in the process of moving away from relating to her, although we were not completely, quite finished yet.

Lydia and I, after the night of her housewarming, would get together regularly. She invited me over for dinner time and time again. She made amazing meals for me. Each and every time I showed up and sat down at her table, I was enthralled by the creations she would prepare. I felt I was being 'wooed' by her phenomenal food! Well, for me, that was very good. Yes, the child in me felt very nurtured and supported, indeed.

At our dinners, we would mostly just sit around and talk, and, eventually, we very naturally fell into making love. By mid-summer, Lydia and I had gotten pretty serious.

I decided the next step for Lydia and I was for her to meet my parents. We organized a weekend to drive to Toledo, and took her green '72 Chevy as transport. As soon as we arrived, the parent connection I witnessed was phenomenal. My mother, in particular, just fell in love with Lydia.

It was an easy task, to be fair. Lydia was the kind of person who was very warm-hearted, and so she made herself right at home, engaging easefully with the family, and helping in the kitchen to do what she could, even washing dishes after dinner.

"Oh, Mrs. Meredith, what can I do?" My mother was taken with her.

Watching this unfold sparked something inside me. Up until this point, Lydia and I had been *just friends, just friends, just friends*. I was starting to consider, however, that perhaps it was high time to solidify our relationship, and take some solid steps to do so.

After our weekend with my folks in Toledo, Lydia and I talked about it, and decided to date exclusively from here on out. Only problem was, I was still figuring my way out of the other relationship. I think Lydia knew, but she never bothered about it or started anything, which spoke volumes to me about her character.

Here is a young lady that I connect to conversationally, personally, spiritually, and really well physically. I fell in love with her. It was too easy. Later in the summer, I popped the question, and she said, *Yes!* And life was good.

Nobody at church had any way of knowing that we were engaged, so we decided to continue to keep our relationship separate from the church, and not yet allow the two to fully overlap and integrate. After we married, Lydia revealed to me that she had actually taken counsel with the pastor right after we were engaged, and that he hadn't possessed approval for our marrying whatsoever. He had reservations, though I've never known fully what exactly those were.

Once we did announce our engagement to the church congregation, we were just starting to plan out our wedding ceremony and reception. So many parishioners offered to fulfil certain duties of the wedding for free as they came around to congratulate us that - as we were both such avid parishioners ourselves and were beloved amongst them - what would today be a $30,000 wedding, was basically donated by our congregation.

They were all so incredibly supportive, and Lydia and I felt absolutely beloved and celebrated. And life was good.

My entire family from Ohio, and Lydia's from Macon, Georgia were in attendance, and it really was the wedding of the year! It was beautiful, we had a wonderful time, Lydia and I loved each other, and... *life was good*.

At the time, I was still working my job at the TV station, while Lydia worked as an engineer at U.S. Steel. As she had a new home, and I did not, and I had a lot of furniture, while her home was still quite barren, we fluidly wove our lives together. We set up shop, and lived like a nice little married couple.

I wanted to start having children straight away, as it was important to me to be sprightly enough to run around and play with my children once I had them. Lydia had no objections, so we started right off, working on children!

We were married December 3rd of 1978, and our first son was born in November of 1979. We didn't waste *any* time.

The day my son was born was by far one of the happiest of my entire life. After his birth, I would just hold and stare at him, nonstop. Something had shifted in me, and the caregiver surfaced. I first took on the role of a nurturer with my son. My sweet boy, Dennis Taylor, named after myself and after my grandfather's last name.

Next thing you know, we're going after another one! A year and ten months after our first son, came the second one. My second son was born February 11th, 1981, and we called him Micah.

And *life was good.*

Now here we were, this great little family. I was doing well in work, and our family was close and cozy. It was then that I decided I wanted to go back to school. I was a minister, yet I hadn't ever formally studied religion, the Bible, and all that it pertains, so I wanted to become a more astute preacher by going to school. Lydia agreed to support my decision, so I attended Samford University in Birmingham full time while she went to work, making a decent amount of money to support the family intermittently.

In the late spring of 1981, I was called to be a Pastor at Mt. Zion Baptist church. I was thrilled to the brim about it! Here I was, in school full time, married, with two children, and now pastoring this medium-sized congregation, to top it off. Whew! Life certainly *was* good.

My graduation from Samford was a huge deal, as I was the first of my family to graduate from college. I graduated with a Bachelors of Arts (BA) in religion, and a minor in speech and the dramatic arts.

Lydia had finished her masters at Vanderbilt University in Business Administration years earlier, so it was yet another very exciting time for our family, for me to take the next step in my own career like that. And life was, again, so good.

Buying cars, and just living a life full to the brim with beauty.... I did have to get rid of my motorcycle after the children came, to avoid the risk of leaving my beautiful new family, but I was more than happy to compromise to ensure I'd be around to support them all.

After my graduation from Samford, I decided I wanted to go to grad school as well. As Lydia was fully in support, I filled out the applications, and was then accepted to a school in Mill Valley, California. In order to determine whether it was God's will that we transfer to California, we agreed, "If Lydia gets a job, it would be a sign that God is sending us to California."

As it turns out, Lydia did get a well-paying job as an engineer at PG&E (Pacific Gas and Electric), a utilities company serving the Bay Area as well as parts of Southern California. The job would provide for our family while I, again, attended school full time. And as a matter of fact, PG&E ended up paying for our entire move across the country! God was prosperous in supporting our transition, indeed.

Before the move, we bought a brand new Chevy diesel van to drive cross country, so I left Birmingham by myself a few weeks early to do so. I stayed in student housing while awaiting Lydia and the kids' arrival. Here we were, now moving from this big 'ole house into this small, two-bedroom apartment in student housing.

We made it work in our tiny, new apartment. I was in my first semester at school when I heard about Mt. Calvary Baptist church, a vacant church nearby in Oakland, California. I decided to try out for the church. They asked me to preach a sermon, and I was then interviewed by the deacons, trustees, church staff, and members of the church, to see if I was a good fit. I indeed was, and was soon after called to pastor the church.

Watchnight, the first of January in 1985, I started pastoring at Mt. Calvary. It was a fairly good, large church, located in a converted old movie theatre, comprised of about 350 members. The church had a solid membership, and a really good feel to it.

Unfortunately, I had to drive from Mill Valley, where we lived, out to Oakland, where the church was located. It was a long commute. And as Lydia worked in the city of San Francisco, she too had a fairly long, significant commute each day.

After finishing my first semester, and getting called to pastor Mt. Calvary, I decided not to return to school again in the spring. The way I saw it, my ultimate goal with going into seminary was to get called to a church, and here I was, in my first semester, having been already called to a church! I had already achieved what I had set out to with school.

At the start of 1986, Lydia realized she was pregnant once again, and nine months thereafter, in October, our third son, Eddie, was born. We really weren't expecting to have any more children, but little Eddie was perfect and we embraced him with all the love we had given to our first two sons. I was, once again, the elated and happy father.

Lydia, because of her weekday commute, would have to leave an hour before she needed to be at work. Her days ended up being ten to eleven, sometimes twelve hours long, depending on the traffic. Though I, too, had a fairly long commute, I could make my own hours being the pastor that I was, and was thus able to spend a great deal more time at home with the boys during the week when Lydia was gone.

I basically lived the life of a stay-at-home father, and became the nurturer of the family through that time. Of course, I loved it. I was the nurturer, I was the father, I was the everything.... I cooked the food every day, raised the children, took them to the doctor's office, and drove them to and from school. Clothed them, fed them, transported them, cleaned up after them. I did it all.

Lydia was their go-to homework parent. She supported their studies fully, always arranging to help them when she arrived home from work. And on weekends, she would cook these lavish, wonderful breakfasts the phenomena cook that she was, and she would fry fish, make some grits, pancakes with peach compote. Ah!

We were still living in our two-bedroom apartment, only now with three boys, and one of them a baby. It was surely getting pretty tight in there, so we found a house located in an upper-middle class neighborhood called Grass Valley. We made the move, and life was just phenomenal. And definitely, more spacious.

Then, in 1987, I was granted the opportunity to travel to Africa on a preaching mission for a whole month. Lydia took some time off to take over some of my caretaking duties, as well as her usual responsibilities, while I toured Africa. I made some friends out there, one of whom became my very best friend after we returned. I felt so grateful for everything God had graced me with, and life felt incredible, day in and day out.

I loved planting flowers, and had this gorgeous backyard behind our home, where I was able to nourish a growing flower garden. On Saturdays, I generally went to home depot for any supplies I needed early in the morning, and would then spend the rest of the daylight hours gardening. The boys had decided to come to Home Depot with me one Saturday, while Lydia stayed home and cleaned up.

When we returned home, Lydia was sitting at the dining room table, with something held in her lap. She greeted the boys, and told them there was a surprise for them in their rooms, because she needed to talk to Daddy. She needed to speak to me.

Lydia held up the thing she'd been holding in her lap. It was a video tape… of straight porn.

She asked me, "What is this?" in this stern, harsh, demanding voice. "You are a pastor. You are a preacher. What are you doing, looking at this filth?"

I thought, *Ok, I am busted.* I thought I had hidden it well enough for her not to find. We had this entertainment center in the living room, and I had hidden the tape way at the top, behind some speakers, far too high up for anyone else in the family to reach. When Lydia was cleaning, however; she used a ladder to get up and dust behind the speakers, and found the tape set up there.

When I was young, my father had porn magazines stashed all over the house, so I was rather comfortable with the habit of the secret I'd kept from her. I was numb to what I was doing, I'd been doing it so long. I started looking at porn at such a young age, it was just something I'd always done. I did figure she would never approve, and thus never told her about it.

Well, now she knew. And instead of spending my Saturday in the garden, Lydia and I spent the entire day arguing. She tried to convince me that it was something I should not be doing. She thought porn was sinful... I didn't see anything wrong with it. I had grown up with it, and it was just something that I didn't feel was wrong. But it went on and on, as each of us tried to bend the other's will. Matter of fact, we ended up fighting non-stop until about four the next morning, Sunday, when I had to head to church and preach!

After a sleepless night of fighting, Lydia and I decided to bury the issue for the time being, woke our kids up, got ready for church, and headed to church in silence. After service, we came home, and ate dinner as if everything was normal. Even up until Monday morning, Lydia and I simply went through the motions of our routines without engaging with one another face to face again.

I couldn't take the normalcy, and was ready to face the music. I didn't want to live in secrecy any longer. I decided to call Lydia.

She was at work, so I made it quick. She answered, and I said into the phone, "If you are ready, I will tell you everything. There's more to it than just the porn."

She swallowed loud, and returned, "Yes.... Well, I will be more than willing to talk when I get home."

SEVEN

THE MARRIAGE PART TWO: FALLING OUT

Lydia returned home from work later that day, and we shut ourselves in the dining room, where we knew we couldn't be overheard.

I told her everything. About my affairs with men, that I was bisexual... everything. It was 1989.

Twelve years into marriage, three kids later, and here I was telling my wife that I identified as a bisexual man. And I probably wouldn't have told her for a long while longer, had she not found the tape I'd hidden.

It's not that anything was missing from my life, save for the open recognition of the truth of who I was; who I'd always been. And the truth was that having sex with a woman - even copious amounts of it - doesn't keep you from feeling attracted to men. And never feeling quite able to tell my wife the truth about my sexuality, well.... I was tired of the secrecy. Of hiding, pretending, and going through the motions of trying to cover up my full sexual expression, as though there was something wrong with me. It was as though I had been living with the broken arm my whole life, exhausting myself to keep face; to pretend everything was fine. And it was exhausting... to live that way.

Lydia and I even had a phenomenal sex life, too. It was great! For me, we never really had quite *enough* sex, as Lydia would often deny me when she wasn't in the mood, or I would desire it more than she would, but all in all we were incredible together.

Thing was, after I told Lydia everything, she didn't really even seem angry. She seemed... disappointed. I had expected her to demand a divorce, and push me out of her life. When I originally called her at work earlier that day, I figured that today would be the day I would need to get out of dodge. That I would need to leave my current lifestyle, pick up the pieces of my life, arrange to see my children, and otherwise try to navigate through all by myself.

But no. Her response to me was, to my surprise, "You are a good husband. You are a good father. You are a good lover. And therefore, we will work this out."

Honestly, when she said that, I was blown away. I never expected her to be so *accepting* and *understanding* of something that seemed to me like an earth-shattering betrayal. For I felt it was a betrayal, an ultimate betrayal, but that it was just how I had lived for so long, and no one had ever 'found me out' before. Because of this, I was somewhat looking forward to the simple relief of being able to come out as a bisexual man. I was hoping to get off the hook, and to be able to live a life of fully standing in truth.

I had grown so tired of living in secrecy; of living what felt like a double life. I had known no other way, however; and was ready to answer for everything, however the chips were going to fall. But for my wife to be supportive, and loving, and ready to heal what was broken... I had prepared no part of myself for the opportunity to actually fix things between us.

I knew I loved her, I loved the kids, and loved the life we had built together. I didn't really *want* to have to leave to figure my shit out, and now that I was provided the option, I quickly pounced on it. *Maybe I'm not really gay,* I thought. *Maybe I could find my truth, and live a life of honesty, without having to give up everything I love,* I thought, pondering what it would mean to stay and be held accountable for the affairs, the porn, and sex with men, and then said to Lydia, "Well, obviously let's figure this out; we can work this out. Things are not that bad between us. We can fix this."

*We **could** fix it,* I figured. Not understanding, at the time that your sexuality *is* your sexuality, and that there's no fixing anything about it, I decided to stay because I felt like maybe it could be fixed. Maybe I wasn't homosexual, maybe I was just broken. Perhaps I was confused. But perhaps I didn't have to run away from what I had, and give up everything I loved, all because I had been keeping these secrets from my wife. Maybe there was a way to stay and be happy.

So after some pretty heavy, consistent dialogue about my sexuality, we decided it would be good for us to see a therapist. Due to my public prominence as a pastor in Oakland, Lydia and I decided it was important to keep our situation a secret.

Yep, that's right. We were planning to kill one secret with another. So we looked for someone with whom we figured it would be easy to fly under the radar of my church's awareness. We had to find someone we could trust with the privacy we had hoped to keep.

We decided to look for somebody outside of the African American community; somebody Hispanic, White or Asian, so they hopefully wouldn't have any correlation or overlap with my church's interwoven communities. We planned not to disclose that I was a pastor to our therapist, once we found one, but still didn't want to risk the possibility of exposure.

We found a therapist whom we believed, by the sound of his name, would most likely not be in the circle of the communities who could associate me as a pastor of the church. Unfortunately, we walk into the office, and this guy is black. After purposefully searching for somebody *outside* the African American communities of the Bay Area, Lydia and I were stunned at the irony of our situation.

Since we'd made the appointment, we had to follow through. Taken aback as we were, we gave the session a shot, and shared our story and struggles with the man. After we'd spoken for some time, the gentleman turned to Lydia and said, "Well, your husband is who he is, and what you're going to have to do is to decide whether or not you're going to live with it, because this is who he is. This is his sexuality."

I hadn't quite realized it in the session, but by the time we made it out and to the car, Lydia was seething. Her anger exploded, she was mad as all hell, since she'd been anticipating the therapist to say that I could be delivered from this propensity towards men, or I could somehow do something to "solve the problem" and no longer feel the way I did.

Lydia started pouring out her anger, spitting it in every direction, shouting about how the man was no Christian, was not of God, and does the work of the devil. She could not accept his opinion that perhaps my sexuality was not up for discussion, and that I simply was the way I was. Lydia had fully believed it in her heart that somehow our therapy session would reveal the pathway towards my no longer being a bisexual man, but it just didn't go that way.

As we sat in that session, and I heard the man say to Lydia "you've got to decide whether or not you're gonna live with it", I didn't say anything, but I was elated! I was pleased with how the session had turned out, pleased that perhaps there really wasn't anything wrong or broken about me, but I was too scared to say anything to Lydia. I was scared she would give up, and I would have to leave. I was scared she would just start another fight about it. I was scared, too, that perhaps the therapist was wrong, and perhaps there was still something wrong with me. I was just too scared to address the issue.

In the meantime, in her quest to find a way around my sexuality, Lydia discovered the Merrimerth And Mire Clinic in LA. A clinic that deals with people who have and live with addictive behaviors. She said, "I'll tell you what. If you go there, this will save our marriage, and I think we'll be fine."

She had read some literature on their methodology of intervention tactics and success, so she was trying to intervene. I agreed to go, and a few days later hopped on the motorcycle I had convinced back into my life, drove five hours to this clinic in LA, checked myself in - her insurance covered my expenses - and got ready to try my darndest to stop being addicted to being gay. Basically.

From the perspective of those treating me at the clinic, there was something wrong with liking men. I could only like my wife, because that's the way it was meant to be. Their therapy was all engineered around banishing my desire for the same sex. Just like Lydia had hoped for.

So after being in the clinic a few weeks, my therapist told me he wanted to prescribe me a drug that would reduce my sexual desire. I instantly got the chills, thinking, *Mmm, this doesn't feel good, it doesn't sound good, and it is not something that I want.* I called Lydia after speaking with the therapist, and told her what they wanted me to do. As soon as she heard that they wanted to reduce my desire for sex, she said, "Oh, no no no! You come home. Do not take no meds, cause I don't want them to interfere with our sex life. I'm not willing to deal with that. No. Check out. Come home." So I did just that.

On my leave, the clinic gave me a list of therapists in the Bay Area who we could contact and work with to further my recovery from being a gay bisexual. When I returned home, Lydia and I went down the list of therapists together, and decided on a therapist *all the way* across town in, Palo Alto. Again, hoping for the therapist to be detached from our African American community, hopefully not recognize me as a pastor, and therefore protect the exposure of our communal struggle.

Unfortunately, God has a crude sense of humor sometimes. In our approach to find someone outside the African American community, we walk into this office, and again cannot ignore the irony in finding an African American sitting behind the desk - a woman, this time.

Despite our frustration, Lydia and I settled into giving the session all of our attention, and this time ended up satisfied with the results. Our therapist diagnosed me as a sex addict, and Lydia as a workaholic. She said that the reason I engage in sexually promiscuous behavior was because Lydia's work made her absent from the marriage, and so long as she was absent, it granted me license to engage in sexually promiscuous behavior with men outside the home. She said, "You're doing this kind of dance, where you go back and forth. Lydia has work, Dennis has sex outside of the home."

She went on to say, "In order to get healthier, you're gonna have to get to know each other and become friends all over again." So she recommended that there be no sex for a month.

Funny thing is, we turned that advice into a game, where I moved into the other bedroom in the house and Lydia was in the master bedroom, and we would sneak into each other's rooms on a regular basis through that whole month, still having sex. We would of course go to that therapist and say, "No, we didn't do anything." But she and I never stopped having sex, because we had a really good sex life, and really thrived in that area.

We continued to see the same therapist for about a year and a half. We saw her together on a regular basis, and then she would see Lydia by herself to address her personal issues, and me by myself, to address mine. In one of my sessions, the therapist recommended that I should work to have a deeper bond with another man. Yes, this was the common advice for how to "cure gayness" in the late eighties… to set a gay man up with another man.

I'll never forget when she said, "Now, this will help you. What we need to do is align you with a man who can become a friend to you, because you need strong male bonding, and that will help you to not like men."

She aligned me with another guy who was a therapist, who could befriend me while working with me on not being gay. So we'd go out on a Friday night to a sports bar, and talk about football and all that. And mind you, I *could not care less* about football, or about sports of any kind. I remember sitting there at the bar, talking to this therapist-friend about football and sports and thinking, *This is awful. I hate this. I don't even wanna do this.*

I went back to the therapist and told her what an awful time that was for me, so instead she recommended I join this organization called Exodus, that works to help men not be gay. Sounds crazy to say it nowadays, but this was the way the cookie crumbled back then. And I went! I would walk into these meetings, set up very similarly to what I know an AA meeting to look like thanks to Hollywood, and we would sit in a circle and take turns talking about what we had done, confessing our mishaps, and helping each other through.

I gave it a shot. Really, truly I did. But as I sat there, listening to these men regretting their choices, something in my mind, heart and spirit said, *This is absolutely ridiculous. I can't even take this.* So I left after a few sessions, never to return, which didn't really matter anyways, since the organization soon after fell apart, as the founder of Exodus was still practicing sex with men all along, and only pretended he didn't.

Well, *all this effort* to try to stop me from being gay, or stop me from liking men, and if anything, it had the opposite effect. After all these experiences, after all this time, I'm here trying to save my marriage, do what I thought at the time was the appropriate thing to do, and consciously change the way I feel about men, but even still, it doesn't stick. Even still, all along as I'm doing this, I'm still having sex with men, I'm still engaging with men, and none of this averted or stopped or prevented me. It did not work.

In the early nineties, Lydia and I finally came to a reasonable conclusion. That I was not able to change, and that I was still attracted to, and wanted to have sex with, men. In fact, I still remember her distinctly saying, "Well I understand who you are, just do not bring anything home, and do not get me infected with any kind of disease." She basically just said, "Do not put it in my face."

Lydia had come to a place of acceptance about who I was. She saw that I couldn't live without exploring the side of myself that desired men, and basically gave me the *OK* to be myself without needing to leave her and our kids to do so. She was willing to bend, and to make it work so that I could be myself, and I really appreciated how difficult that was for her.

As a matter of fact, at one point, Lydia even bought this book about bisexuality, I can't remember the name, and she sat me down and showed this book to me, asking if I wanted to bring another man into our home, or into our relationship. She straight up just asked me if I wanted to, in case that would satisfy my passion and desire for sex with men.

I did not, by any means, want to do that… I thought, *Ohhhh, no.* As I was so used to my sexual secrecy, it was embedded within me not to share this secret sexual desire. I was at the time entrenched in this practice. There was some relief in my life, now that Lydia knew everything and we could be open about it, but still the secrecy provided a cloud over me. One which I could not seem to penetrate.

You know, it's hard sometimes to see through our habits to other ways of being and seeing the world around us. Our perceptions determine our reactions and responses to what happens in our lives, and so we do have some choice as to how we make the kind of life we want to live. But I for one get so clouded, so easily, around old baggage. Old stuff can blind me to my options; deep-seated fears will make it seem impossible to feel anything other than fear. And I feared the changes that were being presented around me.

I just wanted to feel good, and to be comfortable with my life, now that I had gained some freedoms from the guilt, shame and secrecy of my early life. I wasn't even able to see that some discomfort was bound to occur, if I really wanted to live the life I felt inside I wanted to live. I feared that the changes would be things getting worse, instead of better. So I tried to stick to the edges; keep to the status quo - factually, I didn't have to try, really. It was the persevering habit of my unconscious self.

Nevertheless, I knew change was gonna come. It always did. So I figured it might be the right time to make changes where it felt a bit safer to do so.

Now we're late into the year 1992, and Lydia and I are discussing the possibility of leaving California to move to Atlanta, as Lydia's side of the family still lives in Macon, Georgia. She wanted to move back, close to her family again. I was excited about the chance to move closer to my side of the family in Ohio, as well, since my folks were now getting older and it became more expensive each year to fly back and forth, what now with three children in tow. After going back and forth about it for a time, we came to the agreement that we would move to Atlanta, if and as it was aligned with the Lord's divine timing.

In my search for jobs, I noticed an appealing, vacant church in Nashville, Tennessee. I sent them my resume, and quickly began dialoguing with the pulpit community to orchestrate an opportunity to meet the congregation and preach during a Sunday service, as part of the interview process.

In the meantime, Lydia and I were set to spend a sunny weekend in New York for the National Baptist Convention, so I asked a friend of ours to look after the house while we were gone for the week. We decided to add a few days to our trip, and fly from New York to Atlanta for the weekend, to check out the city and see how we felt about it. The woman who was watching our house just so happened to be there when a man named Charles Airs called. She told him we were spending the week in New York, then set to fly to Atlanta for the weekend, and Charles told her that he just so happened to live in Atlanta, but was in North Carolina for the next few days, visiting a friend.

Charles was a musician at our California church for a short time, during which we became friends, but since he left the church and moved to a different city, our connection had become somewhat more distant. I really hadn't heard from Charles in quite some time, but I called him back to see what was up. When I did, he said to me, "Well, I understand you're in New York at a convention," and I told him I was coming through Atlanta shortly thereafter, so he said, "When you come through Atlanta, give me a call, I'll show you around and all that."

He decided to cut his North Carolina trip short, just to show us around and take us out to dinner. So, although Lydia and I were reluctant and really just wanted to explore the city for ourselves, when we got to Atlanta and settled in, I gave him a call. It was early in the morning when I told him where we were staying, but he came over immediately after breakfast, insisting we get in the car with him to travel around more easily.

As soon as we got in the car, Charles starts in on his pitch, "Atlanta would be a great city for you. You're a great preacher, great pastor, and you'll love pastoring here. So the main reason I wanted to connect with you was to show you some vacant churches in the area."

Lydia and I looked at each other sideways, thinking it a strange coincidence he should mention us moving to Atlanta, since we hadn't told anyone, apart from each other, that we were thinking of moving in the first place. Strange, that he would start this conversation without knowing we were there to get a feel for the city; to potentially live there.

So we quietly let him take the lead - let Jesus take the wheel - and the first church he took us to was Tabernacle Baptist Church. He said to us,

"This is vacant. This would be good for you." as he led us into the church. We walked through, and then went directly into the basement, where the church's Fellowship Hall was located. After we walked into the hall, the first two people we met there were the chairman of the pulpit community, and the chairman of the deacon board. Charles introduced them to us since he already knew them, as the chairman of the pulpit community was also the choir director.

He told them who I was, and they walked us around the church, still not knowing that I was even interested in moving there. They asked me if I would visit service on Sunday, so I said, "Yes, we would be happy to consider visiting tomorrow, to see what the service and the people are like."

When we left that particular church, we went and visited two other churches in the Atlanta area. At one of the churches, I met yet another member of the pulpit committee. Afterwards, we had dinner with Charles, and he then dropped us back at the hotel.

Lydia and I got settled in for the evening as we discussed which church to visit the next morning for service. We were undecided, so we slept on the decision. The next morning after we woke up, when we discussed it, both she and I mentioned feeling something special from the visit we'd had at the Tabernacle church.

"I think we should go back to Tabernacle and visit that church." So we got dressed, and went to Tabernacle that Sunday morning.

Once again, I had an occasion to speak with the chairman of the pulpit committee, Ralph Mitchell. He asked me, "Do you sing? Are you one of those singing pastors?"

And I said, "Well, yeah, I'm one of those singing pastors. I do sing."

He then said, "Will you sing for us today? Will you do a solo?"

So, I was sitting in the audience like the average worshipper - wasn't even in the pulpit - when he called me out, to ask me to sing. He said, "We have a guest preacher in the house today, visiting Atlanta, and I understand he's one of those singing pastors, so we want him to sing for us!"

I got up and sang, and the response from the audience was just... overwhelming. They received my singing so well, they started into significant praise and shouting. It was incredible. I had never seen or felt anything like that before! If anything, it harkened back to those days of singing in church as a young boy, performing in the plays and such. I felt more deeply affirmed than I ever had before. I felt *celebrated*. And I wanted more.

After service, Lydia and I packed up and hopped on the afternoon plane that would take us back home to Oakland. Monday morning, I made an attempt to call Charles to thank him for his hospitality, but couldn't reach him. He didn't answer his phone, but later on that evening, I received a call from a friend of mine in the Oakland area, who said, "I just want to let you know. You may not have known, but Charles Airs died Sunday."

I said immediately, "What?! We were *just with him* on Saturday!"

Apparently, he died of a massive heart attack in his car after he finished playing the organ for the church he worked at. He was only forty-two. As soon as I told Lydia what had happened, we were both aghast at the irony… that, out of nowhere, this guy calls us, not knowing that we were even coming to Atlanta, much less planning to move there. Then he drives out of his way to show us around and tell us what a great city it would be for us. He shows us some churches, the first of which is the Tabernacle, a church we immediately fall in love with. And on top of that, the first person he introduces us to is the chairman of the committee, which provides me the contact to then be called up there to sing at Sunday's service.

Absolutely everything about our meeting was synchronicity, serendipity, and irony! And then, the same Sunday, I worshipped with this magical church he had introduced me to, he isn't even there, but is working at another church he didn't show us, just before he has a massive heart attack in his car, and dies. As though God had used him, in his last moments, to connect me with this church, just before his life was over.

Well, that sealed the deal! We were obviously meant to move to Atlanta, and I don't think God could have provided us with clearer signposts that it was just exactly what was meant for us! I mean, it was just the eeriest feeling that crept up my neck as I heard the news of Charles' passing. Lydia couldn't believe it either.

After our visit to the Tabernacle, they did not stop reaching out and calling me until I agreed to preach for them for a Sunday. They paid to fly me out there not just once, but a couple of times, to preach and to meet the pulpit committee and to conduct the interview.

In the midst of this process, Lydia and I had a conversation about where to move, as I had still been working with the church in Nashville all the while. After she weighed the positives and negatives of each church and location, I interjected, and told her, "You know, I just *feel something* with this church in Atlanta. I feel like they're gonna call me, so I already told the people in Nashville to take my name out of the running for pastor."

Lydia said, "What are you doing? They have not even voted on you or called you to the church in Atlanta yet!"

I said, "Yeah, but I feel like that's where we're going to go. That's where we're going to be."

By the end of the conversation, we had made up our minds. We were going to move to Atlanta, no matter what. So in preparation, Lydia quit her job, and received her severance package from PG&E (Pacific Gas and Electric). It paid her a whole year's salary of nearly $100,000, which we planned to live off of, until one of us found work in Atlanta.

I flew back to Atlanta by myself, found us a brand new home, and we were all set to move, when - don't you know it - the Tabernacle church calls me!

So we moved to Atlanta. The Tabernacle church had been vacant for some time, and so much was in disarray. The people were hungry for effective and good, strong leadership. So we had a lot of work cut out for us when we first got to the church, and since Lydia was not working at the time, she decided to start working as the church's secretary.

And then, on April 1st of 1994, was my first official Sunday service, preaching to the congregation.

EIGHT

THE CONFLICT

All this time, in my marriage, I had been saying that "life was good" with Lydia and the children. And it really was. Even with the somewhat recent changes in our home life and dynamic, we still had a really good time together, even when we were struggling.

Now, once we got to Atlanta, I could start off by saying that "life was good", and really it was for a time, but once Lydia started working as the secretary to the church, life became *not so good*. She and I started to have these really intense debates about the church when we were at home. Her working for me quickly became an unexpected source of conflict between us. I guess it was too much strain on our relationship working in the same space together. We had two different leadership

113

styles, and as a result would argue needlessly about which way to go, regarding some of the more important decisions.

Remember, too, that Lydia had received a master's degree in business management from Vanderbilt; whereas, I only had a Bachelor of Arts in religion. So her management skills, while I did value and appreciate them, often caused rifts and conflict between us. It was quite challenging. Things grew so tense and uncomfortable between us at the church, having to wait until we would get home to grind into each other about the issue of the day.

The church Tabernacle had an extra space in the basement they were renting out to a woman who was a member of the church and ran a daycare out of there, called Teddy Bear Day Care. Lydia would interact with this woman from time to time, and after observing her and the daycare for a short time, approached me about it. She felt that the childcare was in deplorable condition, basically running as a babysitting service. In Lydia's observation, the childcare needed a lot of careful attention.

One afternoon soon after, Lydia's sister, who also lived in Atlanta, asked her to join in on a class she was taking to become certified to work with children in childcare. Lydia was free in the evenings when the class was taking place, so she decided to take the classes and became certified.

While taking these classes, her observations of the Tabernacle church's childcare became only more and more robust. The information she gained from her certification course only added fuel to her fire, and she would constantly share with me just how poorly the childcare was being managed. She affirmed with me how it was not up to code nor in line with the rules and regulations for the state of Georgia, which I eventually realized was, all along, the lard she had been using to butter me up in anticipation of asking me whether she could take over the childcare.

I consented, saying, "Well sure, so long as you're sure it's something you really want to do."

I've never really denied my support for Lydia, in following her aspirations. Never attempted to keep her from things she wanted to do. So I said to her, "Well, go ahead and take over the childcare, and I'll get somebody else to work as church secretary."

As soon as I said it out loud, I recognized the added bonus, that perhaps this change in position would rectify our tensions; resolve the constant conflict we'd become lost in both at church and when at home. As soon as she switched, it did help the cause, and she would still offer to me her expertise in business and management, when I told her about the situations I had to solve within the church. Only now, without the added personal momentum, and I was free to again fulfil the role of a good listener, happy for my wife's supportive advice.

I was happy for a time, hoping we would no longer have any need to fight and debate over topics related to the church. The problem then became, however; now that Lydia had taken over the church's childcare, she wanted to expand it. She approached me at home one day, saying, "Well, I don't have an office in the childcare, so can I share your space with you?"

Yes, it was true that my office was rather large. Her idea was for half of the space to be taken up by my office, and for the other half to house her necessities for running the childcare. I believe the right idiom here would be to *not bite the hand that feeds you*, but sure enough, once I agreed to share my space with her, she ended up taking it over, and pushing me out! I had to move out of my original office, for the job I had been given by a church in a city we had recently moved to, and into a random space upstairs, on the third floor of the church. I felt like I had no choice in the matter. I mean, she had filled that basement office to the brim with documents, and toys, and other things for the childcare, and it hadn't taken long.

All in all, this move of mine happened about two years after we moved to Atlanta, in 1996, and it only took from the time we got there and I got settled into working with the church, until 1996, when I felt like her position as Director of Childcare, which I had given to her, was already superseding my own!

So now it's more like, *Eh, life is just OK.*

I thought to myself, *Well, at least she's out of my hair now. She can go ahead and run that childcare all she wants.* I didn't think things could get any worse with the situation. *But,* I was wrong. Surprise! The childcare only expanded more and more and more.

She licensed two more rooms in the church to fill with child care, then she licensed Fellowship Hall so the kids could have more opportunities for activities. Soon after, she licensed yet another room, at which point the childcare was then taking over a greater portion of the church than the *actual church*!

As this expansion was happening, Lydia and I were experiencing terrible conflicts about it. Members of the church had started to approach me, saying, "We don't have any space for the church, because your wife is taking over everything."

So now I'm caught in the middle, between allowing my wife to utilize this space, and the church members feeling as though children's stuff is everywhere, and there's now no space for the adults of the church!

Lydia and I were battling about this problem, constantly going back and forth, and all the while, she continued to license new rooms and expand the church's childcare. I couldn't believe what was happening. I wanted to stop Lydia, but I felt steamrolled over, unable to get it across to her that what she was doing was quite ridiculous, and was actually ruining some of the things we originally fell in love with about the church; that made us want to come here in the first place!

Well, even still, I would say my peace, and Lydia would expand the childcare. At this time, the church purchased a pretty significant amount of property that surrounded the grounds. Lydia saw this as an opportunity to push my office completely out of the church itself, and into a nearby house that the church had recently bought, situated behind the church.

I wanted to object, and I did object, but my words proved powerless to Lydia's aspirations. I just thought to myself, *Well okay then. Lydia can have all of that space. She can have the Fellowship Hall, my old office, all of it... and I will just move.* I went peacefully, I really did. Even though I knew what she was doing was wrong, and completely out of control.

And sure enough, when the church purchased another property, a duplex nearby, Lydia came along and licensed the whole thing, turning it into yet another space for childcare! Honestly, how many children need care in one church? Really, there weren't even enough adult members making children to make use of any of it!

Well, she and I just fought, and fought, and fought, and fought, until I finally said to her, "Lydia, listen. This is killing me. This fighting. I just cannot go on fighting with you like this."

For some reason, perhaps somewhat due to the fact that Atlanta was a town rich with African American people, and perhaps also in response to my conflicts at work and at home, soon after we'd moved to Atlanta and settled into the city, my connection with men, and with my bisexuality, just escalated, and went to a whole nother level. More detail on this...

We had decided it was best for us to go back to counselling. We just couldn't seem to get along. Well, the therapist helped us to see that her workaholic behavior had escalated as my sexual addiction behavior escalated, and we both just got tremendously worse in response to the never-ending conflicts we had been facing again and again.

One thing that bothered me, though, which I mentioned to our therapist, was how I felt Lydia's addiction was a more accepted, and even perhaps applauded addiction, as it resulted in perceptible success; whereas, mine was deemed more disturbed, and nasty, and ugly, and useless and... so on, in common society. It seemed unfair to me that, if we were both addicts, one of us seemed to have more of a reason to be acting into their addiction.

In fact, what the therapist revealed to us in response to my remark was, "An addiction, is an addiction, is an addiction. And you don't say one is worse than the other, because they're all thieves to anybody or any relationship. When you have an addiction, it robs you of your happiness and your joy, and it robs you of being able to have a healthy relationship and a good family context."

So we were, both of us, addicts, then! And that's all there was to it. Each attempting to handle our emotions and issues through instant gratification payoffs rather than through putting in the hard work. Each escaping the present moment, the reality of our lives, instead of staying with the discomfort and pushing through.

And that was it for me, really. I was *tired* of changing myself to fit into something that just... didn't seem to work any longer. Didn't seem to have any joy left, to be frank. The conflict, the tension at work, the fighting at home had all just become more and more intense, to the point where I could no longer function in the marriage.

I remember, one afternoon, we argued so severely that it took everything I had in me not to become physically violent. Of course, with the childhood I had, I have never and would never let myself *go there*, but boy, was it tough to not grit my teeth straight through my jaw that day! Lydia got right up in my face, and she just screamed at the top of her lungs, like a wild animal. She called me a male chauvinist, and forced my actions into this corner of having been *intimidated by her feminine strength*. Mind you, Lydia worked in corporate America, and then worked with me, all the while we were married, and I never disapproved or tried to put the kibosh on any of it. So I really struggled to see myself as what she'd painted. But she just said "It's all your ego. You won't let me do this."

The work-church-home conflict between us grew to be so bad, Lydia finally ended up searching for an alternate location, and then filing to move the childcare out of the church. Sadly, this was an unfortunate solution, as moving the childcare out of the church was actually moving the children, as the childcare, for the Tabernacle church, was a beacon of hope and light for the entire community. That community we were in was made up of families with children who attended the church and then also went to the childcare.

I remember saying to Lydia, "If you move the childcare out of that church, you're moving out of my life, because this childcare and the church together have been in this community for a number of years, and that union has been a beacon of hope and light for this community."

The church was right in the middle of a government subsidized housing project. So, to come into this community, providing accredited, quality childcare, and a church that is very family oriented, was really a benefit to the community. For her to build up the program as she did, only to then pull this church completely out of the community, out of the neighborhood to another facility, was to remove a vital resource the community members had built their livelihood upon!

But she insisted. She said, "I am moving, and that is it." And then she moved the childcare out into another space that was not too far from the church, but was no longer directly a part of what was known as the Old Fourth Ward Community - the neighborhood the church was in.

The church never knew anything about our conflict, since we'd worked so hard to keep it confidential, but when Lydia finally ended up moving the childcare out of the church, my prophecy came to fruition. She moved out of my life when she moved the childcare. Our marriage was over.

I'd always said "life was good" for us, but really, life was no longer good for us. Life was no longer good for me, and Lydia was greatly shocked and surprised that I was actually moving on.

We made the final decision to separate in August of 2006, but I had honestly, probably checked out of the marriage about five years before that because of the conflict between us.

Remember how I said I was a master at keeping secrets well watching porn was one of my kept secrets. I never mentioned to Lydia about my addiction to porn.

I actually started looking at porn at a very early age. It carried through into my adult life. I got interested in porn from looking at magazines my father had hidden throughout the home I was raised in. My father had several magazines they were under his mattress where he and mother slept. There were magazines in the bathroom hidden behind the tub. There were also magazines in the night stand next to there bed. I remember how I would be so happy when I could be at home along so could go into the bathroom pull out some of those magazines and masturbate. I am certain that my brothers found the mags and was doing the same thing. By the time Lydia discovered the porn in our house I had had years of engaging in watching porn. So when she confronted me it was a bittersweet moment.

Bitter because now I am caught and my secrecy has come to light. I was really out of control with this porn watching. It was on a regular basis that I watch gay and straight porn. I had a lot of free time on my hands. The boys were in school all day and Lydia was at work all day. I hoped that her finding out would help me to curtail my porn issue. Once again growing up in the Meredith home there was no condemnation issued out around pornography. I vaguely remember my mother speaking to my father about making sure he hid his stash well enough so me and my brothers would not find it. But I don't recall my mother condemning my father for his porn mags. By the time Lydia found the porn in our house I had had a long history of looking at porn.

All in all, our marriage did not end as a result of my being bisexual nor my sex with men. We traversed that. We changed to allow for it. Nor did it end because of her addiction to work. The marriage really ended because she and I just did not get along, in the end.

We continued in the marriage for sixteen years after I opened up about my sexuality. Mind you, my children never knew anything about my struggle with my sexuality during the time. They knew only of how I was a good father and a good nurturer.

To me, it was clear my sexual addiction was not the reason the marriage had come to an end. Rather, it was the fighting, over and over again, over leadership styles in the church.

Lydia put $3000 down on a condo in a community called *The Enclave*, because she had decided to move out. She was planning to move out, and get her own place, while I would remain in the new home we had recently purchased.

In the interim, before she moved out, about four months after we had decided to separate, I met this wonderful man, Lavar, and began a relationship with him.

One of the most refreshing things about having this relationship with Lavar, while still married to Lydia, was that he was not a part of my church, and thus there was no discussion about church, and absolutely no need for any similar conflict. *No* debate about the church!

I felt so free to be myself! Lavar and I were just enjoying ourselves, going out to eat, and doing things that normal couples are known to do. So our relationship continued to grow, somewhat as a result of just how fun and free it was.

As one man entered, one woman exited my life. Lydia and I had enjoyed a really good sex life for a really long time, but *the fighting* just took away my desire to want to be with her. Stole away my affection for her. After we started working together at the church, it was just no good. Just a downhill thing.

Some people today believe it was Lavar, my husband today, who had caused the demise of Lydia's and my marriage, but I didn't even meet Lavar until November of 2005, when Lydia and I were already in the downswing our relationship.

The following year, in May of 2006, the condo Lydia had been preparing to move into, I ended up taking. As it turned out, after she discovered I was involved in this relationship with another man, she decided, "I'm not giving up my house. This is *my* house, and you will have to leave."

So I said "OK", and I moved into the condo.

NINE

BEING DIAGNOSED AS A SEX ADDICT

After I'd opened up to my wife about my sexuality, we started seeing

a therapist, in an attempt to figure out how to live our lives in a healthy and prosperous, wholesome way. It only took the woman two visits to conclude that I was a sex addict. That was her prognosis; her diagnosis of my struggle.

One of the things she recommended, so I could more clearly come to understand what sexual addiction looked like, was to read a book called *Out of the Shadows* by Patrick Carnes. I got the book and read it, and my wife read it as well.

Upon reading the book, it was clear to me that the patterns I was living - the behaviors I was exhibiting - made it apparent I was a sex addict. Although, I don't think the therapist's diagnosis was exactly... comprehensive. In other words, I thought it only revealed one side of the problem, and quite frankly, only a very narrow view of what my true struggles were.

Throughout our sessions together, the therapist never mentioned anything about the chance that my self-esteem issues could have something to do with my addiction. Yet later on, as I got older and started looking into why I might be promiscuous, I realized that it very clearly came from a great lack of self love. But it was never mentioned, and I recognize today that this whole ability to provide therapy to people who struggle with different things, addictions, or whatever the case may be - that the whole approach to dealing with the human mind is still an evolutionary process... it is still evolving.

In hindsight today, I don't believe that the approach of how the therapist was dealing with me in attempt to eradicate this addiction I was struggling with - or suffering from, depending on how you view addiction - was an approach that could put me on a path to better manage this sort of out-of-control sexual appetite I had developed.

I saw this movie recently called *The Danish Girl*, which was about a a guy who was married, yet in the midst of his marriage, discovered that he was suppressing the fact that he felt as though he were a woman, but in a man's body.

Once it all came out into the open, and he realized with clarity just what he had been suppressing, he couldn't go back to suppressing it any longer. He could no longer ignore the truth he had recognized, and the more he got in touch with that area of his mind and body and soul, it became very clear to him that he was supposed to be a woman, even though [s]he had been born a man. This story was inspired by two Danish painters: Lili Elbe - one of the first recipients of a sex reassignment surgery - and Gerda Wegener, and their true life together.

When Lili Elbe tried to talk with a therapist about her rising feelings, every single person she met with said she was insane, and that she could do nothing about it, as she had been born a man. The only offered practice, from psychiatrists and doctors he met with, was to go into her head and cut off certain parts of the brain, as well as exhibit shock therapy treatments. And really, these methods were only in attempt to completely eradicate her feeling of truly being a woman.

No one wanted to accept Elbe's emotions as truth, and yet that's just what they were: *her* truth. Nothing was ever wrong with Elbe *except* for believing that anyone else would know more about her than herself. No one can know or understand you better than *you*. And even though doctors and therapists have degrees, and credentials, they no more have the secret to life's puzzling riddles than does a cat, or a circus clown, or a dry cleaner, or a homeless LGBTQ youth, or you, or me.

Seems to me this is one of life's greatest illusions: the idea that there is someone out there better suited to know you than *you*. We put all our faith in external things, when really, what we need to do is put faith in ourselves, and who we know ourselves to be.

Not every leaf looks the same. Not every flower buds in the same way, with the same color, at the same time of year, or even with the same reproductive parts! There are always discrepancies. To me, this is nature. To me, we are a reflection of nature - a part of it - and thus, we are made in its likeness. We are nature, each blooming organically in our very own, unique way, and in our own time; adding beautiful facets to this kaleidoscopic world as we do so. This is what makes life fascinating, and beautiful.

That's why I say, when you look back in time, at how long and often choosing to be gay has been regarded as wrong, or sinful, it's just been a waste of time. There's no reason why we can't evolve and choose to live in ways which may never have been chosen before. In fact, I feel it is our absolute purpose here, to do just that! To choose fresh ideas, and new ways of thinking and living... no matter how long it takes society to catch up!

We've evolved so far, as a society, past what was once perceived; we've progressed so far past such antiquated thinking towards the mind, and the body. And yet, up until the late sixties, lobotomies were still performed! Shock treatment is still issued to individuals unresponsive to "formal' treatments. It makes me scoff, and want to puke, and laugh in the face of its ridiculousness! Perhaps we should try approaches more outside the box, in a more loving and "coming into your truth" kind of way, rather than resorting to the use of outdated therapy treatments that only harm the body and the mind, more than help it.

We do not live inside boxes. We do not live "formal" lives. Life isn't formal, and never will be. Life is messy and raw and real, and we are free, no matter who tries to put us in cages, or stuff us in little boxes that limit our true potential.

Just recently the conclusion was revealed, that for person to try to reverse their sexuality - especially in any invasive way, such as through the mind - can cause irreparable damage. And here I was, not forty years ago, being told the exact opposite; being led down just that very path.

What I did, rather than do what the experts told me, was learn to follow my own instincts, and live in my truth. No longer to choose secrecy for the sake of others' comfort. I recognized just how resolute I had to be, in not listening to what the world thought of what made me happy, in order to live the life I wanted to live.

The therapist tried to cure me from being gay. The doctors tried to cure my cancer. Neither of those things worked [apparently]. Neither one of them tried to help me *heal*, to become whole again.

The therapist never once tried to help me deal with these risky sexual practices that I was engaging in, that were violating the trust of my marriage and putting me at risk, because of how I was behaving when it came to having sexual encounters with men while married.

My issue is in how my therapist didn't really deal with my issues. She was a Christian-based therapist, and she simply tried to solicit her personal, religious views and push her personal interpretation of the Bible onto me. To me, it was kind of sad that she took me down a path that really didn't help, and down a path that, for all practical purposes, does not lend itself to changing my sexual orientation.

The idea is also tragic to me, that you can go to a therapist for help, or really anyone for help, and that the person who is supposed to be supporting you chooses their own truth above yours. They use their truth as a means to get you to see things their way, rather than support you in finding a healthy outlook and perspective on *who you are*, to support you in developing habits that align with living a more healthy and joyful lifestyle. [For the way you want to live it; for what health and joy mean for *you*.]

Unfortunately, I believe my therapist's approach was from the vantage point of, "I'm going to tell you that you are a sex addict. But since you are having sex with men, we need to cure that; rather than help you understand or make a connection with these risky behaviors around your sexual practices, or help you try to come to terms with accepting who you are."

The entire time was, to me, just a misdiagnosis: It just wasn't right. The approach was not supportive, nor healthy. It didn't help me, except to see more clearly that I should truly trust myself before another.

The evolution of human sexuality is critical to human understanding, because we are evolving. We are always evolving, and we will never stop. It is our nature. Hybrid plants are often created to survive harsher conditions, or simply to shift with the changes of the ecosystem they live in.

We are, as a society, on the path towards coming to a better understanding that, when it comes to human sexuality, it is as fluid as our own natures, and that you just cannot put it in a box. Yet there are so many still living in the old ways. Still prescribing old treatments. Continuing to push their own beliefs onto others, rather than provide guidance and truly helpful support.

As a matter of fact, my work with the therapist only caused me to become more secretive about my behavior, as though my fears had been realized, and that there really was something wrong with me and my desires.

Would the therapist have dealt with the real source of the promiscuous behavior, or the real source of what was *really* going on - my low self esteem - then perhaps I would have made progress, instead. But that was not the therapist's objective. Rather, it was this whole: "If you have sex with men, or if you're gay or bisexual, that's what we've got to deal with." So face value, when really, it was not what needed to be dealt with.

What I needed from her was to receive support in cultivating a greater sense of self awareness and self love. So that, even if I was going to continue being bisexual, or go on living in a marriage where I was a bisexual man, at least I would have been more aware of my source of low self esteem, and then been able to work on answering the question, "How do I love me... enough to not put my family at risk, nor put my wife at risk, nor put myself at risk, nor even my church, and live with a greater sense of accountability?"

And now, this was 1989. In hindsight, obviously this particular therapist had not recognized some of the findings of the times, as, in 1973, the American Psychiatric Association voted to no longer consider homosexuality a mental disorder.[2] As well, in 1975, the American Psychological Association took the same action.[3]

So here I am in 1989, after these findings have been publicly released, dealing with a therapist who is - after also having sent me to the

131

Merrimerth and Mire Clinic - trying to cure me of same-sex love. When truly, all long, it was never even something that needed to be addressed in the first place, and only stopped me from getting to the true heart of the matter.

Truth is, when I look at the secrecy and pain of my life, my work with the therapist only enhanced my pain; it only enhanced my secrecy. [Perhaps why the subject was awarded it's very own chapter!] Instead of finding within myself the ability to transcend my low self esteem, the sessions sent me to an even darker place.

By the time I got to Atlanta in 1994, Lydia and I had broken away from that particular therapist, after having been with her for five years. *That's right*, sometimes, it takes a long-ass time to recognize your inner voice. But once we got to Atlanta, I was just *really* out of control. I mean, really, really out of control with my promiscuous behavior. I was in a much darker place in Atlanta, than I was even in California.

I refer to this promiscuous behavior, over the years, as having been a time where I was in a very, very dark place. So dark that I could not see my way clear out of it up until I had my epiphany [where this story begins] over a decade later. That's when the light finally came on. Something inside me snapped, saying, *Enough is enough!* The lights had finally been turned on within me, bright enough to wash away all the darkness, saying, *You have to do something different with your life, or you're going to pop! You're going to die, you're going to pass.... There is no other way.*

This therapist, diagnosing me as a sex addict only to put me on a path to *eradicate* my homosexual behaviors, had put me on the wrong path. It was not helpful. It was not healthy. And I guess I have to say, you have

132

to be careful who you see, as a therapist. You have to be careful with whom you trust, whom you seek support from, and whom you let into your world.

I get really concerned, nowadays, when someone approaches me and says they are Christian, because that means, to me, that the way they think is skewed in a way that may be against certain people; against a population of people. The mindset doesn't generally seem to be supportive, or open, or inclusive in nature... more, close-minded. Though, of course, I recognize how no one is *ever* limited by their religion, sex, choices, or any of that. I merely developed a defensive recognition with Christianity due to the deep, deep pain that was caused because of this one therapist, and her refusal to help me actually heal. I believe she saw my sexuality as wrong, or demonic, which only made me see myself the same way through our time spent working together.

Rather than being receptive to help people live healthy, live free and live out loud in who they are - without being shoved in the closet - many therapists, or "helpers" can potentially lead you down a path of darkness, where it is then only your own sense of right and wrong that can help lead you away from those who wish to do so.

You know, you see these therapists with all these other terminologies for different "disorders", which only cause you to feel - or make you think of yourself as - "less than"; like less than a human being. This approach only compounds the problem of not loving yourself, as it was in my case. Of not embracing your truth, *whatever* that is. For me, it only compounded the problem, causing my secrecy become more secretive; the pain of my secrecy only more painful.

133

I think something has to be said about this. About creating boundaries for what perspectives you let through. What you allow in, to affect you.

One of the books I've picked up since, which really opened my eyes, was *Jesus, the Bible and Homosexuality: Explode the Myths and Heal the Church*, by Jack Rogers, a professor of theology emeritus at San Francisco Theological Seminary. [He's also the moderator of the 213 General Assembly of the Presbyterian Church.]

The Presbyterian Church chose Jack Rogers to write a book about the Bible and homosexuality, as they had wanted to give a definitive statement on why homosexuality is not a sin. And of course, they chose perfectly. Rogers is so profound in his explanation of the Bible and homosexuality. He speaks to how the Bible does not, in any way, prescribe the notion that homosexuality is a sin, and notes how, even though the church has, throughout the ages, attempted to use Bible passages as a means of oppressing marginalized groups, there is no passage in the Bible to support the claim that any one person deserves less than another for acting on who they feel they are inside.

I've always believed, period, that the Bible was never meant to be, nor should it ever be, referred to as a textbook on human sexuality. In the end, this perspective only causes people to repress, live in secret, and even commit suicide. Really, it causes *so much pain* to the human condition when someone skews the Bible say something it does not, or uses it to feed their own homophobic ideas, when it's not even about that!

Was I a sex addict? Well, I probably was. But to be diagnosed as a sex addict and be told I need to be cured of my homosexuality: That's two different things; they're not the same thing. All in all, I needed help. I needed support. I needed understanding, and love, and ideas to help me formulate my own sense of self love, so that I would stop seeking it so aggressively from external sources. But did I receive that? Any of that?

No, I did not. But I did, eventually, find and give to my*self* each and every one of those things, and without guidance, mind you.

Just imagine what progress we could make if those who held positions of power; positions meaning to lend support, helped us love ourselves more deeply, and helped us to actually shine a bright light on the darkness within.

TEN
LIVING AS A BISEXUAL MAN

After the divorce with my wife, the Tabernacle church went through a period of decline in membership, as many of the members had originally seen us as - you know - the ideal family: husband, wife, three children, living what you would call 'The American Dream'.

When it came to our family, I can see how everything on the outside probably looked perfect; like the perfect representation of a united, faithful family. Of course, on the inside, however, there was trouble in Zion... there was *trouble* in the home, as you are now well aware.

My now ex-wife - as they called her: Sister Meredith - had captivated the congregation. People had a real affection for her, as well as a deep appreciation for what they'd imagined to be *the* example of a strong

137

family dynamic presented before them. I could see how it offered inspiration, from the external, to see our big family all together like that; so faithful. They had placed hope in our family simply because of who we were, and what we presented on the outside.

The inside was so very different. We didn't mean to deceive; had no intent as such, but we did choose to keep our business as *our* business, at least until such a time as the changes in our family unit would need to be publicly known, affecting the image others held for us.

When I ultimately decided to come out to my congregation, some members were very disappointed, either because of our divorce, or because of my announcement of coming out as openly gay and living with a partner. What surprised me, though, was how it wasn't only heterosexual members who were offended by my coming out. There were many openly homosexual members who were offended as well; who apparently didn't want to accept my being openly gay.

I do believe they left, truly, because they felt deceived. Perhaps betrayed. I see clearly how I had been presenting one image in front of them; while in truth, there was another life I was living. A life I didn't have the faintest idea how to come out about, however, as it was never an all-out, black-and-white thing. I was never "gay", or "straight", so much as I was always "fluid". Or in other words: bisexual.

I have lived my life as a bisexual man. Even when I was married; even when I was young, I was attracted to both men and women equally. I found there to be benefits to getting involved with each sex, as well as drawbacks.

Bisexuality, to me, is often misrepresented socially, and in society as a whole. I never intended to - in fact, if anything I went out of my way not to - deceive anyone. Or at least, I held no motives as such. I found it so difficult to come out as openly *gay*, in part because I am not simply "gay", so much as I am bisexual. When I was married to a woman, I felt I didn't fit, quite. And yet, when I was assuming the role of being "gay", it never quite fit either.

As though lost between two worlds, I've tried to find my place; but in my experience, bisexual men, as a whole, do not get a fair shake. I find that bisexual men are more looked-down-upon than bisexual women. Many people seem to be repulsed by men having sex with women, while also having sex with men; whereas, when women have sex with men, but then also have sex with women, it is desirable. Often, female bisexuality even stands as a turn-on, and is socially celebrated.

Not to say that I approve of how female bisexuality is hyper-sexualized in this way. My point is, rather, that it is tough to desire both women and men, as a man, and feel good about yourself in doing so, when there exists this stigma that something is, somehow, *extra* wrong with that choice.

I've been in conversations over the years regarding my being a bisexual man, where the person I'm speaking with tries to convince me that I'm just "confused". They'll say, "Well, if you're bisexual, you must just be confused; you don't know what you want."

I'm not confused. I know what I desire. Sure, it's a confusing world, but I find being bisexual is less about being confused, and more about having the opportunity to actually choose which individual person you want to be with, regardless of their sex. And *then* being confused, when the world tells you that it's wrong for you to do so.

Bisexuality is fluidity. Do you want to be with a male? Do you want to be with a female? You can say which one you want to be with. Moreover, it's not even so much about the sex of the person you want to be with, than it is about the quality of the connection you actually have with that individual person.

In conversation, I have often been greeted by some form of rejection towards my bisexuality. I have, more often than not, received the response, "You can't be bi. You're gay. There's no such thing as a bisexual man. If you have sex with men, you're gay. Even if you have sex with women, but also have sex with men, you're still a 'gay man'."

The concept may be hard to grasp for some. But it seems to me that society isn't helping. I believe, in particular, with our primarily patriarchal society, where men seemingly set society's norms for what is and is not socially acceptable, this whole idea of being able to equally enjoy both sexes is misunderstood and goes unaccepted.

As such, men are somewhat of a major driving force behind what goes accepted and unaccepted in regards to sexual practices. Though I find this to be shifting somewhat more so in current times, I grew up and found myself in a world run primarily by men and their opinions. And let me tell you, what I've learned from what the men of the world have taught me, is that bisexual women are sexy and cool, intriguing, and even beguiling; while bisexual men are repulsive. So, too, then does society find bisexual men nasty, grotesque, taboo, and just plain wrong.

I just find it to be unfair, that this stigma has been placed over bisexual men, keeping them from accepting their beautifully fluid natures.

I've noticed that, even in the gay community, choosing to be bisexual is unacceptable. The community dismisses you. Especially amongst African American people, it feels unacceptable to choose be a bisexual man. Perhaps this is truly the reason why so many members left my church. Maybe they were already too convinced that being a bisexual male was somehow a cop-out, or that it was more wrong than simply being gay.

I feel as though I've never really had a formal place of acceptance, when it comes to my sexuality. Even now, I feel a resistance towards disclosing to people that I am bisexual. Even though I am in a same-sex marriage, and relationship, I am still bisexual. But I instinctually hide it! Even after all my talk of secrecy, and all my coming out, and stepping into my truth, I experience resistance to walking in it. It's difficult not to preserve yourself through secrecy, when nine times out of ten, people don't surprise you, by judging you for your choices.

Much of my community - the circles I run in - is made up of gay men, and yet I will choose to conform; to shy away from sharing that I am bisexual. So many times, have I gotten looks from gay men who are obviously thinking (or say straight to my face), "How could you be Bi when you're married to another man?"

The thing is, my sexuality does not change because I get married. Maybe that's been my main problem all along: That once married, the perception is that your sexuality aligns with your commitments. But it doesn't. I couldn't be a straight man when I was married to a woman. I can't be a gay man while married to a man. I just can't. And it's because my sexuality is my sexuality, regardless of my choice in a long-term partner.

I feel as though I could very much still enjoy the company of a woman, participate in making love to a woman, or being sexual with a woman, even though I am married to a man. Of course, I am faithful to Lavar and choose not to be with women to support my commitment to our relationship, but I still feel as though I'm quite capable of it.

But I don't say it; I don't talk about it. I don't acknowledge it or open up about it. I don't converse about it. *Even my husband* feels like this is an unacceptable sexuality, I guess, or that to be so is inane. So I guess, in a way, I'm still kind of living in secrecy. Just, not as extreme a form as when I was completely ostracizing my attraction to men.

I choose to want to belong; I choose to want to be accepted in my community. And so, this is my own private kind of interpretation of my sexuality. I don't want to say private, but it is something where I don't often open up and discuss. Even though I'm putting it in this book, I just don't open up and discuss it, because I don't think people are accepting, understanding or, want to be inclusive in their ability to place a value on people who are like me; people who are bisexual.

In dealing with HIV, the CDC coined the acronym 'MSM': Men who have sex with men. I found it so interesting that they had to come up with an acronym, as there exists this whole population of men who have sex with men, but would never consider themselves gay. All the same, I find it strange for the acronym to exist, as it means pretty much the same thing as 'bisexual': That you will have sex with a man and you will have sex with a woman. With this whole idea of bisexuality being completely unacceptable, however, I guess that term was out. And thus, MSM is a term many men who do not wish to associate themselves with being gay, or being bisexual, will use. A term to stay under the radar of social red flags.

I can understand it. Of course, you know me and secrecy. We have a long, sordid past. But what I cannot understand is the need for this whole other term to identify this particular population within the gay community, as opposed to just using what's already there of the LGBTQ equation; that being, "bisexual".

I found it to be almost impossible to exist someplace in the middle, desiring both men and women, while making it make sense to me - much less make sense to anyone other than me. Honestly, it sometimes feels as though bisexual men don't exist in our society, and are hushed into secrecy as a result. I've felt this way for so long, and never knew exactly how to share my understanding of myself with others, or whether or how it was even an appropriate thing to do.

I've done, from my analysis, the best I could with the truth of my situations as they've come. I tried to support and find new members, and connect with those who weren't scared away by my revelation, but it proved difficult.

My revelation took a tremendous financial hit on the church. For about six years, from 2007-2013, it was a real, real difficult struggle to keep the church afloat, financially. We didn't have the members, nor the support we'd had previously, and were struggling to make even the meagerest of ends meet.

By November of 2011, we were so far behind in our mortgage on the church that the bank sent a representative out to talk to us about restructuring our loan. They informed us they could not continue to move forward with our being late on payment all the time. The mortgage was around $6,000 a month, and we were not raising that amount of money. Month after month, we were unable gather enough funds to pay the church's mortgage, along with other operational expenses. And unfortunately, you've got to operate the church in order to get volunteers in there, to voluntarily give their money.

The bank offered us a plan where they reduced our mortgage to $2,000 a month, cutting away $4,000 from our regular monthly payment. They offered this plan to us for one year; where after, they would then reevaluate to see if our payments arrived on time, and would consider restructuring the debt, go back to the $6,000 a month payment or, if they could, increase it.

I accepted that plan, and in the meantime, figured I'd search around for a new building for the church. I figured, worst-case scenario, we could lose the building during the course of the year, and have no place to worship. So I planned to find a suitable backup, just in case.

I was looking to rent or buy another building; though, I figured it was more than likely we would be renting as we were so strapped for cash.

The following year, just before the plan with the bank was up, this gentlemen comes into the church, knocks on my door, and introduces himself before asking me who about the ownership of the property behind the church. We had acquired this little house behind the church over the years, as well as a separate duplex and vacant lot behind the church.

I said to the man, "Well, the church owns that property.".

He asked me in response, "Are you interested in selling the property?"

"Well, yeah, we will sell the property for the right price," I said.

So he replied, "Well, I got a buyer who's looking to buy up some properties in this area."

Folks had been buying up a lot of properties around the church at that time, as we were in this major area of downtown Atlanta - the last one that hadn't yet been sold off. There were a lot of older African American people that lived in this community at the time, though they're all gone now as folks have come in and gentrified the area, putting in half a million to two million dollar homes, pushing out the middle class and the older black people.

He said, "Well, I got somebody who'll give you $250,000 for the house."

I tried to hide my reaction. I was floored. We had only paid $30,000 for the house originally, so I said, "Okay, sure."

And though a voice in my head thought it might be too good to be true, a week later this man came back and he said to me, "Well my investor wants to know if you have any more property to sell."

145

So I told him, "Yes, we do actually have another. A duplex and vacant lot. And if you're interested, we'll sell it."

So he said to me, "Well, we'll buy that as well. We'll close the deal here for both of these properties in about two weeks, if that works alright for you."

I thought in my head, *Good Lord, this is good timing.* Here we are as a church, flat broke - I mean, we were struggling week to week to make ends meet, even with the lowered mortgage - and here I've been searching for a new place to move to before the year is up, and this man swoops in with an ungodly solution! Although, I knew it in my heart that this was actually a *very Godly* opportunity, in fact.

So two weeks after, we sold the two properties and had a half a million dollars in the bank. The buyer wasn't even at the closing, yet we walked away with a check for half a million dollars!

About a month later, the agent comes back again, saying to me, "Well, you thinking about selling your church?"

And I muttered to him, "Well, I hadn't thought about it, but for the right price, I'll sell the church as well."

He said, "Well, I think I might have somebody who wants to buy the church."

So we got a full vote of the congregation, and they collectively voted to sell. We went and put it on the market, and he came back with a buyer for $875,000.

Only, now we had to hurry up and find ourselves another building for worship, because these people wanted to move in quickly. So I had to start looking for another church.

I took my partner Lavar along with me to check out this one church somebody had told me was on the market. We got lost trying to find it, but once we did, we pulled up to the gate, and found that it was locked, and we couldn't go any closer. So, Lavar and I got out of the car, took one good look at the building, and then turned to each other, saying, "This is our church. This is our building."

It was perfect. And as history has it now: There we were, flat broke, struggling, about to be foreclosed on, and within less than nine months, out of nowhere, we have $1.2 million in the bank.

So we paid cash for the building that we now own. And though it's not as big as that church was, it serves its purpose, and it's perfect for our congregation. We were able to pay cash for renovations to get it ready, and still had money in the bank! We have no mortgage, the church sits on three quarters of an acre, we have plenty of parking, and just… everything, everything we need. And on top of this, the congregation has since been growing and growing.

So when I talk about surviving a lot, I have survived a lot. When I talk about being able to overcome a lot, I have been able to overcome all of this.

So I don't know. You know, people say that's how God works.

But I'm faithful. And I'm very, very thankful; as right here today, even with all of that: I'm still here.

ELEVEN

COMING TO TERMS WITH MYSELF

I met Lavar on November 14, 2005, in an adult book store where I would go sometimes to rent porn DVDs. He and I chatted some in the store, exchanged numbers, and then the next night, I made my way to his apartment. We talked all night, and had sex into the wee hours of the morning, before I made my way back home.

At the time, when I first met Lavar, Lydia and I were in really bad way. We were separated, yet living together still. Meanwhile, we continued to maintain the public appearance that all was well at home; it was a delicate time. I had been with different guys before, during my marriage to Lydia, yet I had never felt the desire to take things any further than the occasional, chance sexual encounter. A get your fix, and get out. This time, with Lavar, however, it was different. I knew it immediately.

I was in a very vulnerable state of mind about it all. I really wanted something more than just sex with Lavar; I wanted an emotional connection. I wanted to get to know him. Feel what it was like to be with him.

I continued to see Lavar occasionally. We would go to dinner often, and have conversations about the simple things of life that mattered. As he was not in church, our conversations were not about the church or kids or childcare - none of the stuff that had kept Lydia and I uncoupled. It was so refreshing, I was swept away, and within a matter of months, I was in love. I asked Lavar if we could be together, exclusively, and he consented.

By January, when I was diagnosed with cancer, I revealed to him my diagnosis; where, at twenty-seven years old, he further blew my mind by telling me how my cancer diagnosis would not interfere with our relationship.

He said to me, "I'll stick with you, and help you get through it."

His response made me love him even more. This young man could so easily have walked away, and so easily have found someone else - someone much 'easier' than I - and yet he chose to stay with me. I felt so valued and deeply loved by his support. He didn't see me, or all of my baggage [being sick, being married, being in transition with coming out] as any reason not to be with me, and as I had fallen so deeply in love with him, I was further motivated not to let anything come between our love.

Our lives together, in the beginning, were no fairytale story. Those days were very difficult. I had not yet publicly come out, I was a prominent pastor in Atlanta, and still very much a married man to Lydia. I felt I had to keep our relationship under wraps for the most part, even though I wanted to scream my love for him from rooftops.

By May of 2006, I had moved out of the house with Lydia, and taken ownership of the condo she'd originally planned to move into when she was going to leave me in August of 2005. Once Lydia had the inclination that I was seeing someone, however, she told me she would not leave her home only for someone else to move in. She insisted that I move out instead, and I complied. I moved out of the house with only my personal things.

Lavar's and my relationship was difficult, even beyond all my baggage. We were two low-self-esteemed men. I was bisexual, he was gay. What a combination! Two people living with self-hate, yet trying to figure out how to manage a healthy relationship, all the odds stacked against them.

Little by little, people in my life began to discover that I was in a relationship with someone who was not my wife. In the spring of 2007, I decided it was time to come out to my congregation that I was bisexual. Later that summer, I introduced Lavar to the congregation as my partner.

Since then, our love has soared. We learned how to move through self-hatred into a place of self-love. We talked together often of how to forgive our pasts, in order to move forward together, in a sturdy, supportive relationship. We've had so many good times, for all of which I'm more grateful than I can say.

I've wondered, over time, why I was so promiscuous during my marriage, while in my relationship with Lavar, I am practicing and living a monogamous life without complication. I've discovered a lot about myself, in reckoning with my past, and changing my present to align more with a life of openness and loving awareness.

One of the major differences between my marriage to Lydia, as opposed to my marriage with Lavar, is in how we have developed a stronger system of accountability. Lavar strongly holds me accountable for my sexual behavior, and I him. Under no circumstances do either of us tolerate sex outside the relationship.

We are each too well aware of the sexually promiscuous behaviors of gay men. We also know the source from which this promiscuity comes from: low self-esteem; a lack of self-worth. So many gay men have inferred from society that they should hate themselves for who they are, and there is an epidemic of low self-esteem strewn across the gay community as a result. Lavar and myself have been privy to this, and are much more able to openly speak our truth to one another, without fear of ridicule, criticism, or shame. We are too well aware to do that to each other, knowing it only furthers the problem.

Through social norms and religious beliefs, gay people have been condemned and judged for centuries. The history runs through books and blood. We have been demonized, hated, excommunicated, and even killed for being gay. And unfortunately, the same hateful practices still exist today.

Whenever people are taught to hate themselves or allow themselves to be treated in a way that indicates they are in the 'less than' category of society, it instills in them this belief that they are not good.

Being shamed, and having to grow up in a world where you feel and think of yourself as bad, has a tremendous and adverse effect on the way you see yourself. If you see yourself in society as a person that does not measure up to what the world thinks you should be, you are discriminated against.

Being a minority, in this country, automatically makes you a target and candidate for low self-esteem, and when everything around you reinforces the treatment of being discriminated against, you are at a mental and physical disadvantage for life. [Not doomed, just with extra work to do, to source self-love and worth from the inside out.]

I believe black people, in general, suffer from low self-esteem because of the hatred we have had to endure for so many centuries. Again, strewn across the histories, through books and blood alike. We are a population of people around the Globe who are still trying to rise up and transcend the decades of being mistreated.

Now, when you are black *and* gay, you have even more of rough road toward healthy self love. Not only are you black, a social strike against you, but if you're gay, as well, that's another strike against you. Black, gay men, especially, are more disliked and unaccepted than most. So then, the black gay man has not only two strikes against him, but three.

And if he is an effeminate, black, gay man, he is treated even worse than the masculine black gay man. So now you have a black, gay man who treated with disdain and discriminated against because he is black, because he is gay, and because he effeminate. I won't even add bisexuality as a precursor to this list; you get the picture I'm sure.

I am a black man who grew up in a world where I could not escape the traditional beliefs of what our society thinks of gay people. Of bisexual people. My own sense of low self worth kept me, for years, in an unhealthy place, both mentally and physically.

The second reason why I am in a much better place, and have developed a greater sense of self love through my relationship with Lavar, is because of all the hard work I've done to move beyond my self-hatred and habits of promiscuous behavior. I've had to weed the garden that is my soul about a million times over. Till and re-till the soil, and then plant new seeds in the dead of a harsh winter, in the hopes of seeing them rise anew. I had to nurture those seeds like wounded children, urging them to grow in what felt like an inhospitable environment.

After dealing with cancer the first time 2006, I wanted to completely rehaul how I was living my life. For me, this meant no more hiding. I had to live the truth of who I was, and no matter what. That meant that I had to put away the shame, and put it away for good. Reject it if it came anywhere close.

I had to transcend my self-disapproval. Had to fully own who I was, and I needed to do it out loud. This meant self-disclosure, and speaking my truth publicly. Preparing my garden to grow took a lot self discipline, and a great deal of being held accountable by my partner.

My growth has paralleled somewhat to the current shift in how America has approached its own growth, in acceptance of the LGBTQ community. I have been a part of the interweaving of new stories, shifting the paradigms of old to align closer with walking in kaleidoscopic truths.

Living in Atlanta has been especially enlightening during these times. Atlanta is much more inclusive, surprisingly enough, than San Francisco ever was to me. In my humble opinion, Atlanta is one of gayest cities in the country. There being such a large population of the LGBTQ community living here, has made it safer to come out and live your truth.

I have experienced so much love and affirmation from gay and straight people from the communities I dwell in here in Atlanta. I am surrounded by a community that has greatly helped me to be free. To free myself, and feel validated in doing so. I am a completely different person, than the man I was when I was married to Lydia. I have come to terms with accepting and owning my truth, and taking full accountability for my actions and influence on the world around me. I love myself enough to want to live a much healthier life, no longer putting myself and others at risk.

Today, I possess a different value system for what a relationship means.

I once read an article in a magazine that headlined, *Relationships Save Lives*, and encouraged gay men to settle down and find love. The idea was to get into a serious relationship, with accountability, to reduce promiscuous behavior, and thus reduce HIV infection rates - which is still very high among black, gay men. What's truthfully behind this epidemic, however, is a current of low self-esteem, and runs right through the gay communities.

But we cannot play victim to a society that has not taught us the value of self-love. Should we do so, we only stand to spread the disease, incurring the devolvement of gay people everywhere. When we can fix our sense of self worth, and align with the truth that we are all worthy of love - no matter what - it will help to correct a lot of the unhealthiness of our community.

I sometimes cannot believe my transformation since meeting Lavar. My connection with him has taught me the true value of a committed relationship; the true value of such a deep connection. The right relationship can make all the difference, helping you to illuminate an aspect of yourself you were afraid to bring forth in other connections.

Not to say that any relationship is *bad* - no. I find each relationship teaches us, and leaves us golden nuggets of wisdom about ourselves and the world. But the right person surely does make the difference, and has the potential to absolutely transform the way you relate to the world.

Relating to Lavar has been a dream. We have overcome every struggle and hardship, and instead of letting things tear us further apart, they have only stood to bring us ever closer together.

TWELVE

WHAT BEING FREE MEANS TO ME

B eing free to live my life openly has been akin to being released from prison, looking back at the facility that housed me, and saying, "I don't ever want to go back there again."

The freedom to live my life out loud is so rewarding and so powerful. Nothing I've ever known compares to the joy I feel in not having to hide who I am any longer.

Last year, I was invited to attend a meeting at a Christian university, along with a group of other black pastors from the Atlanta area. The president of the university addressed the group at luncheon, informing us on how the school wished to hear what we needed from the university, in order to support our needs. The university was also hoping that we pastors could help to shape the University's Christian curriculum, in line with educating students that would then go out into the world to build good, healthy churches.

I was sitting at a round table with nine other pastors. At one point in the session, the pastors were given a chance to respond and to ask questions. I raised my hand and announced that I was an openly gay pastor and wanted to know if the university president would come to my church and speak to the congregation. My hope here, as I expressed, was in sourcing out potential candidates from my church to receive a formal education on religion at the university. Of course, none of the other pastors had known I was gay until I said so.

As soon as I said it, a hush and cold chill entered the room. The president responded timidly by saying he would like to speak privately to me, but did not openly respond to my question. It was clear, at that point, that I was an object of isolation and alienation. Prior to the president addressing the group, we pastors had all been sitting around, talking, and sharing stories about our churches.

When the president finished speaking, he invited us to go to a buffet and serve ourselves some food that had been prepared by the school staff. I got up and went to the buffet to fix my plate. When I returned to the table to eat, none of the pastors who had previously been sitting and talking with me returned to their original spots. They had, rather obviously, chosen to sit elsewhere. As painful as it was to experience this moment of not being accepted, I had mixed emotions.

While it did not feel good to be so openly rejected, there also surged within me feelings of pride, power and courage. I was happy and proud of myself, to be gay man, in the room, who spoke up openly for his community. Even though I, more likely than not, didn't move the needle of change even an inch in regards to their perspectives on the LGBTQ community, I had made it very clear that I was not afraid to live my truth in front of them.

In that moment, I represented a movement that's changing the world. I stood up for myself, and lived fully immersed in the truth that my epiphany had supported me in fully embracing. Why should I hide who I am for others' comfort? Why should I change to suit others' preferences? There is no need for the secrecy, or even for subtle shifts to save face.

I stand with my community, and am proud to carry them all on my shoulders, to the best of my ability. I imagine the LGBTQ community as a tree with endless branches, and where I used to be a broken, thimbly little twig, barely hanging on, I am now a pillar of my truth. I am proud to be a sturdy branch, knowing that every ripple continues outwards endlessly, past our perceptibility.

This what it feels like to be free. To stand firm in what I know to be true, and right, and integral for all. None of us deserve to hide in the shadows, or blend in with the crowd. We deserve to shine bright, be brave, and engage fully with our voices to sound out our particular, unique frequency, color, shade.

Now, I don't go around with a sign on my chest that says, "Hey everybody, look at me: I'm gay!" But when in a safe arena, and the opportunity presents itself, I will speak up. I do speak up. There have been many times since then, and before, where I was the lone gay pastor, and instead of nestling into the corners of comfort, I have chosen to stand proudly in dead center, choosing to make my voice be heard. And not once; not ever do I regret it. I walk away from each experience and visualize the possible outward ripple, as the potential for change fills me up with pride, power and ever more courage.

You free yourself by recognizing all of the options you have for yourself, and your life. You live in truth by allowing that truth to shift with time and experiences. You live well by being honest with yourself, and even as that truth shifts, doing whatever it takes to live by it.

I didn't *do* this. I didn't actively choose this truth for myself. It simply existed within me from the start. I tried to hold on, and fix something I had always felt, deep down inside, was wrong or broken, and could be fixed...

...but you just cannot fix something that ain't broken!

THIRTEEN
LIVING YOUR BLISS

In February of 2014, I was approached by a local producer who had come to my church to ask me whether I would be interested in participating in a reality tv show featuring preachers. I agreed, and in the following month, signed a contract with the entertainment company producing the content for the series.

After my initial interview, several months passed by before I was notified that, instead of playing a role in the preacher series, the producers thought it would be better if I had my own family show. So in July of the same year, right before my oldest son Taylor got married, the film producer got together with another company, who then both met with my entire immediate family, including my partner Lavar. By then, Lavar and I had been together nine years.

The cast consisted of myself and my partner Lavar, my ex-wife Lydia, and my three sons: Dennis Taylor, Micah (and his partner BJ), and Eddie, my youngest son. We completed our interviews on film, after several hours of filming way into the middle of the night. The whole process lasted from 8pm on a Friday night until around 3am the following morning.

After a few weeks of editing, the producers created a teaser to send to various networks, to see which network would buy the show. Several of the networks were interested, but WE TV jumped on it immediately, offering to buy the show from the local Atlanta producers. By September of 2015, the producers had a contract in hand from the network. After the two companies producing the show received the contract from WE TV, they got into a disagreement as to who owned the rights to show and how they were going to split up the credits once the show aired. The argument between the two producers got very intense and lasted for at least four months. In the meantime, WE TV was consistently on them to return the signed contract, so they could start filming and have the show ready to air along with the other new shows being aired on their network. Finally, and after much fighting, as well as my having to mediate between the two guys, they came to an agreement.

We all - the entire cast - went through the rigorous process of getting an attorney and negotiating with the network our salaries for each episode. Once we agreed on our pay, it was on. By the spring of 2016, we were filming for the sizzle reel. All went well; we completed the filming in about a week. It was quite involved and a lot of work. However, after all was said and done, and after signing contracts with another film company the network used out of LA, the heads of the network could not come to an agreement on airing the show.

I was told the reason the network could not come to an agreement on airing the show was because of the gay issue. The fact that I was an openly gay pastor seriously caused pause for them because they did not want the backlash of haters to flood their disappointment over airing a show with a gay preacher as the headliner.

So the reality show never aired, even though the two local producers continue to shop the show. I think their fighting and the rejection was more than they wanted to deal with, so they parted ways and the opportunity was dismissed. It was actually very exciting though to be considered and go through the process learning what it really looks like to produce reality tv.

I learned a lot about the world even through that "failure" of an experience. And now I see how, really, every failure, or fallout, is really just another stepping stone along the journey of one's path. Being a part of that process taught me a lot, for instance, about how to create and build a book, and present a story to the rest of the world.

I am thankful to be here, taking each and every step, putting one foot in front of the other, and knowing that each step I do take – whether or not it ends in "failure" or "success" – creates an impact on the earth as a whole.

I'M STILL HERE

Come out, come out wherever you are! Whatever your secrets! Whatever your fears! Once you recognize that nobody can harm you without your consent, you will see that you *are* safe and loved. You are perfect and divine and although, yes, the world can try damn hard to hurt you, we are here on this planet to heal. To heal ourselves, and to heal one another into wholeness.

Find community. Find a support system that will let you, and help you to feel your pain, and give you the tools to heal it. To heal the wounds of being bullied, not being accepted, being confused about who you are and what you want… I *p.r.o.m.i.s.e. y.o.u.* there is a reason for every season. We move closer and closer into a wholly, healed earth, the more we heal ourselves and one another.

Times are changing. Heck, the Age of Aquarius is upon us! Remember that musical, *Hair*? Now is the time to own your power, recognize the truths in your heart, and step into the love that will heal up not only the wounds, pain, fear, guilt, or remorse you walk around with, but will *ripple outward* to others as they meet you and hear your story. This is what I'm doing here, with this book!

I've healed myself, and now it's your turn. I pass the baton. I know in my heart you can do it! That is, if I can do it, you can do it. And you will.

It's not fun. Well, if you can learn to laugh at yourself, it can be fun. It's not always easy, but the struggle and the suffering are the illusion. These limitations are false! You are *always* free to make the choice to be yourself. Sometimes, it just takes adverse experiences, gritty times, and a whole heck of a lot of emotions to help you find your way back to your true self. But you will do it. And when you do, it'll feel like falling into bliss. Into, as they say, *"a feather-light mattress"*. I promise.

Even amidst all the good times I've experienced since coming out, there have still been challenges. There are always challenges. There always will be challenges to call your soul to the surface, in attempt to bring out your best self. The things that change, however, are how you respond to the challenges you're faced with.

In March of 2017, I went out for lunch to a restaurant I've been to many times before, with my son and my daughter-in-law, yet for some reason, I couldn't ingest a thing. I couldn't eat. The meal was this delicious smoked barbecue chicken, but I couldn't touch it.

My appetite, from that point on, continued to decline. I couldn't eat chicken to save my life, and there were some other foods as well that I just couldn't stomach. I couldn't even smell certain foods; they would make me instantly sick.

By May of 2017, I had gotten pretty sick, what with not being able to eat. So I went to Emory hospital emergency room - that's how sick I was, going to an emergency room - where they performed an MRI upon noticing that my stomach was slightly swollen. All I knew was that I didn't feel good.

They did the MRI; where after, the doctor told me they found some lesions in my liver, and that I had a growing tumor on my spleen that was pushing my stomach to the right. I should've gone straight to the oncologist at that point, but I prolonged my doctor visit all the way to August, wherein I finally went back to get checked.

The doctor told me that, from his assessment of the tumor, they weren't sure whether it was cancer, but that, with the way my body was looking, I was not going to live past March of 2018. So, I did a PET scan, and they concluded that I had non-Hodgkin's lymphoma. Yippee! Here I am again, facing yet another tier to my battle with my body. This particular lymphoma was more lethal than the lymphoma I'd had back in 2006 and 2009. This particular cancer was a lot more aggressive, and needed to be treated as such.

Well, my liver was so damaged because of the lesions, that by November 1st, I had to be admitted into the hospital. They put a stent in my liver to drain something called bile, because it was building up in my liver and causing my urine to be extremely dark - the color of black tea. Apparently, the only way they could correct it was by putting in a stent, so the bile would flow out past the lesions that had formed.

I had lost a tremendous amount of weight in the meantime. I had started losing weight in May, as I wasn't eating, and by December of 2017 I had gone from 250 pounds, down to 175. I had lost about 75 pounds.

Another doctor then told me that I had to treat this cancer, or else it was not looking good for me to survive it. [Again, with the ultimatum death sentences!] But he insisted that I needed to either use their facility to deal with the illness, or go back to my Emory doctors to deal with it.

I made up my mind that I was going to go ahead and get the treatment. The doctors told me that the only way they could really treat this particular aggressive cancer I had was to do chemo to prepare my body for stem cell transplant. So they put me on the track for stem cell transplant.

Around the 21st of January, 2018, I went into the hospital for a week, because the chemotherapy dosages they'd given me were so strong, I had to be hospitalized to handle it.

There was a lot of controversy amongst the doctors as they decided what to do next, since chemo can really damage your liver. They were skeptical about doing chemo because once again, it would have an adverse effect on my liver. So they had to give me other meds to get my liver back to functioning, as they weren't going to give me chemo until they were able to do some meds to help fix the problems I was having with my liver.

Finally, around the 21st of January, I was in the hospital, I received the chemotherapy and was released to go home.

This particular regimen is supposed to be administered to be every 21 days, but the chemotherapy had made me so sick, that my eating challenges were even greater after the chemo. After that first round of chemo, I was losing *even more* weight. I was down to about 168 pounds at this point. I went down from a 38 in the waist to a 32; went from wearing extra larges, to mediums and smalls. That's how small I had gotten!

The doctors had insisted I come back every 21 days, but I was so sick that I told them, "There's no way I could return to the hospital to get chemo after having been that sick". At that time I was *so* sick - from November through April of 2018 - that I had to use a scooter to get around. I literally could not walk without having a great deal of discomfort in my abdomen.

During this time, I first had the idea to write a song called, "I'm Still Here", as, after all that had gone through in my illnesses and loss of weight, I was still hanging on! Still surviving this cancer - this illness that I was struggling from.

As I was healing at home, and working in between sleep on writing some starting lyrics for my song, the hospital and doctor consistently continued to call, telling me, "You have to do this in 21 days. If you don't do it in 21 days, it's going to get worse. You may not make it, and we won't be able to treat you, based on this. We have to follow this particular regiment, because this is the regiment we do whenever we get somebody ready for stem cell transplant to eradicate their cancer."

Well, finally, after you know, several of these calls, I went back to receive another round of chemotherapy in the latter part of February. It had been thirty days, not 21, but I was admitted to the hospital for another week while they did the chemo and I met with doctors and different administrative personnel from within the hospital.

Mind you, after chemo, you're going back and forth, into and out of the hospital, to make sure your blood count is right and to make sure there exist no pressing side effects. So I was just in and out, and in and out of the hospital throughout January and February. Four to five times a week, I'm just back in and back out... in and out and in and out I go like a Merry Go Round through those revolving doors of theirs. Only, this was no ride I had chosen to be on.

The nurses put me on a really high calorie Ensure, as I had lost so much muscle in my legs I could not walk. I stayed in a bed basically most of the day. I didn't go out much, except to go to the hospital. Although, I still went to church on Sundays. I still preached every Sunday. I would take it easy throughout the week and then on the weekends, do whatever I had to do as far as church was concerned.

After they did the second round of chemo, they told me it was time to do the PET scan to see where the cancer was at and what was going on. When the PET scan came back, there was no cancer to be found. They were a bit baffled, as normally, you're supposed to do the four rounds

170

of chemo and then go into stem cell transplant - and stem cell transplant is really, just, even more chemotherapy.

When I first started the process of trying to discover what was going on, my primary care doctor said to me, "When you decide to deal with treatment on this illness go for quality of life, as at your age, that's what's most important."

Going through chemo really reduces your quality of life, so I remembered what the doctor has said, when after those first two rounds, there was no cancer, yet they still insisted that I do the stem cell transplant. Meaning, going through some more very, very rigorous tests to prepare me, along with taking my own stem cells out, taking some medication that would boost the stem cells so they would come to the surface, more chemo... just a whole nother regiment alongside at least a one year recovery time.

There was just a whole lot involved with it, so I decided I was not going back after I saw the PET scan and it clearly showed that the disease was completely gone from my body. I decided I was not going to go back to the doctor, and I did not go back even though they were calling me, insisting that I follow their procedures.

When I asked the doctor why they were insisting on my following this process, even though the cancer was gone, the doctor said to me, "Well, this is what the textbook requires."

I'm like, *Textbook? Really?!*

I had asked them earlier to conduct what they call a 'gene pool study'. They could perform a study on your genes to determine why you get this type of cancer, and what makes it come back and how best to treat it. They didn't want to do that; they said that was not an option for me to do and the only reason I even knew about it was because one of my members, Shane Colbert, worked at Emory in this particular area of research. And she said that, based upon research, if we do the proper research, we might be able to target why you're getting this cancer and what we can do best to treat it.

Well, that was not something they wanted to do for me. So after I decided I wasn't going back, I got back on my holistic regiment of pau d'arco and French clay and water, and started taking it on a regular basis.

Today, I weigh 243 pounds. I've just about got all my weight back. Most of the clothes I had purchased when I was going through my cancer, I can't even wear now because they're all too small. But basically, I'm feeling fine. Basically, I feel, you know, like I'm cured.

So, all in all, I wrote that song, "I'm Still Here" to commemorate the experience. Because in truth, *I am still here!* After having dealt with cancer, twice. After having gone all the way through to the fourth stage of cancer, when we all know there is no fifth stage. After, both times my cancer was diagnosed, it was as a very, very life threatening form.

But you know, as the song says, 'I'm still here'. And I feel like there is still a responsibility and something that I am assigned to do; that I'm called to do. That my life's purpose is not completely fulfilled, because there's yet undone work that is specifically designed for me to do, to accomplish, and to achieve. And at this point in my life, I'm doing all that I can to do that.

If my life is to be used to inspire, to help, and to encourage others in whatever way I can, I will do whatever it takes. Whatever it is that is meant for me to do. Even with the fact that I've gone through cancer, have gone through - my God - so much that I've gone through in my lifetime. Yet, I've survived it all.

I'm still here from the trauma of my childhood, through adolescent trauma, molestation, being married, divorced, living in the closet secretly as a gay man, coming out of the closet, having to face people who thought you were one way and cannot understand or accept when you turn out to be something else, being a gay, black bisexual minority, and having to go back over my tracks when people thought I was straight and then they find out I'm actually bisexual.

To have to answer to all that, and on top of that go through a heartbreaking divorce, and deal with bankruptcy after divorce because of all the money I had to pay to my ex wife, survive that, lose my condo and cars, and all my possessions. As a matter of fact, I came home one day to a note on my door saying, "You no longer own this condo" because I had filed for bankruptcy.

I had to get rid of everything and start all over again, and survive that. Survive going to my congregation, telling them that I was a gay, bisexual man and having to go through the transition of a lot of straight people leaving the church while a lot of same gender loving gay people were coming to the church. Surviving the loss of income of the church because we lost a lot of income; going from $20,000 a Sunday down to sometimes $2000, sometimes $1500, trying to figure out how to make ends meet.

All of that. Just, wow. And at the end of the day, I'm still here.

I'm *still* here.

ACKNOWLEDGMENTS

This book represents the numerous and countless contributions of persons and people who have touched my life in various ways. The list of those people is so vast that it would be impossible for me to name them all.

I not only count those who were positive and helpful but also those who brought pain and grief into my life. I believe nothing is by chance, and that everybody and everything happens for a reason. Every experience is an opportunity to learn.

I have learned many lessons from my interactions with many people. All of which have made me the person I am today.

In the end, everyone matters; even the guy I encounter on a regular basis when I stop at my neighborhood gas station to fill my car, always asking for spare change. He's a beggar on the streets trying to survive. Even he makes me conscious of my own blessings and the importance of giving to others in need.

All this to say that this acknowledgement is to everyone who, over my 65 years of living, have touched my life in some kind of way.

A special shout-out to my husband Lavar, and my children Taylor, Micah and Eddie for their continuous love and support of my growth.

ABOUT THE AUTHOR

Bishop Dennis A. Meredith is the senior pastor of Tabernacle Baptist Church, where his goal is to inspire, educate and liberate. He gained his Bachelor of Arts Degree in Religion from Sanford University in Birmingham, Alabama. He is most known for his leadership and unremitting efforts to promote change for social justice and human rights for all people.

He focuses relentlessly on equal rights for same gender loving people and couples and has become a role model for all people through his messages of hope and affirmation. His church's motto is *"Love and Acceptance"* and stands firm as an inclusive ministry for all people, regardless of race, gender, or sexual orientation. His ministry provides a religious and spiritual covenant for those who have been prejudicially left out of being allowed to worship in traditional churches because of their sexual orientation or social differences.

Bishop Meredith lives in Atlanta, Georgia with his husband Lavar Burkett Meredith.

ABOUT THE PUBLISHER

Smokeblood Publishing is a mythopoetic collective that strives to seek out, absorb and disseminate creative excellence in the written word.

"The whole thing is a weaving of smoke." -Alan Watts

If you'd like to publish your own book, or for bulk discounts, please contact the publisher directly:

IG: @_smokeblood

Email: connect@smokebloodpublishing.com

Website: www.smokeblood.com

CPSIA information can be obtained
at www.ICGtesting.com
Printed in the USA
LVHW021312090720
660100LV00006B/171